AMSTERDAM

Part of the Langenscheidt Publishing Group

4

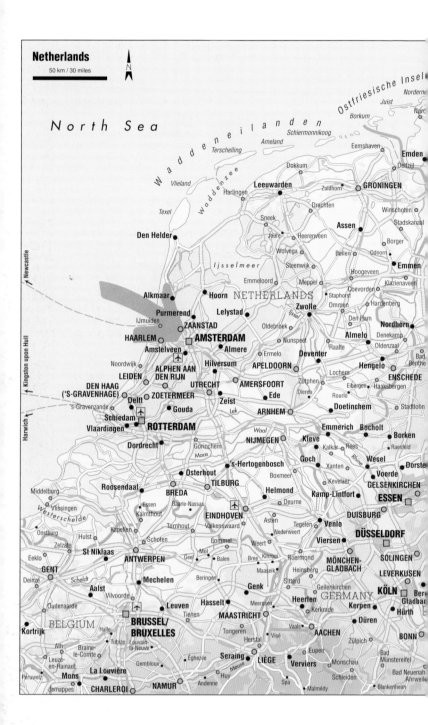

Welcome

This guidebook combines the interests and enthusiasms of two of the world's best-known information providers: Insight Guides, who have set the standard for visual travel guides since 1970, and Discovery Channel, the world's premier source of non-fiction television programming. Its aim is to bring you the best of Amsterdam in a series of tailor-made itineraries put together by Insight's expert on the city, George McDonald.

The guide begins with suggestions for three full-day walking itineraries linking the essential sights. It takes in diverse museums, churches, squares, shops and markets, with recommended stops at cafés, bars and restaurants. A further series of half-day and evening tours cover other interesting areas and aspects of the city, and three full-day, out-of-town excursions explore Haarlem and Zandvoort, the IJsselmeer and The Hague.

The itineraries and excursions are preceded by a chapter on the city's history and culture, and followed by sections on leisure activities – shopping, eating out, nightlife and a calendar of events. At the end of the guide a practical information section includes tips on getting around, money matters and dealing with emergencies, plus a list of recommended hotels and guesthouses at all price levels.

 George McDonald, the author of this guide, is a freelance travel writer who caught the travel-writing bug as deputy editor of the inflight magazine of the Dutch airline KLM. One day he was editing local stories for a newspaper in Britain, the next he was paddling down the River Ganges for KLM. Most of his spare time was spent closer to home, however, in Amsterdam, exploring on foot, by tram, by bike, and in winter on skates, the marvellous city in which he lived.

He says of the city, 'Amsterdam is a state of mind as much as a real place,' and advises you to 'set your mental controls to "open-minded" and "ready for anything", and go.'

In addition to writing this *Insight Pocket Guide: Amsterdam*, the author has also written Insight Pocket Guides to Bruges and Brussels, cities he also knows well, and contributed to *Insight Guide: The Netherlands* and *Insight Guide: Amsterdam*.

History & Culture

W ater is central to Amsterdam's history, geography and culture. The fishermen who first built their huts at the mouth of the River Amstel at the beginning of the 13th century earned a good living from the fertile fishing grounds of the Zuiderzee, although they and their families were at the mercy of wind and sea in that low-lying, swampy delta. Many must have lost their lives as frequent storm tides washed their primitive dwellings away. Yet the community flourished, particularly once a dam was built to hold the Zuiderzee at bay. A by-product of the dam was the creation of a good anchorage, at the point where central station now stands.

Named Aemstelledamme, the settlement soon expanded as a commodities market, to which influxes of Flemish weavers and Jewish merchants made considerable contributions. In 1275 – the year in which the city was officially founded – Count Floris V granted the people of Aemstelledamme toll-free passage on the waterways. This development encouraged further growth in trade. Ships unloaded cargoes of Baltic timber, salt and spices on what is now the Dam, and sailed away laden with cloth, furnishings and grain. In 1300, Guy van Avesnes, Duke of Hainaut, granted Aemstelledamme its town charter. Thirteen years later, Count Willem III of Holland took over the town from the Bishops of Utrecht who had hitherto controlled it. One more link in the commercial chain was forged in 1323, when Count Floris VI named Amsterdam as a toll-point for the import of beer. The city has lost none of its taste for this particular beverage, as a casual glance at the forest of Heineken and Amstel signs testifies, but in the 14th century beer was essential as an alternative to tainted water supplies.

A Phoenix from the Ashes

The pattern of the city's history as a trading mecca was firmly established. Unfortunately the foundations of the city itself were not quite so grounded. Despite being built on waterlogged land, Amsterdam's wooden buildings were vulnerable to fire – and in 1452 most of them were engulfed by flames. In the wake of the fire, the City Fathers ordained, all new buildings would be made from stone. Today, the city has only two wooden houses.

Amsterdam's golden age began towards the end of the 16th century, at a time when Calvinist Holland was fighting to win independence from Catholic Spain. A century earlier, high-Renaissance Florence was the centre of high culture; further back in history the Athens described by Pericles set the standard for human achievement. Amsterdam experienced a comparable

Left: Amsterdam in the first half of the 17th century, when immigration boomed
Right: details of centuries-old gables show intriguing facets of the city's history

burgeoning of art, culture, science and exploration. In the words of the historian Simon Schama, 'There is perhaps no other example of a complete and highly original civilisation springing up in so short a time in so small a territory.' Though its lustre may have been dulled by the passage of four centuries, the glint of the golden age shines through the contributions of subsequent generations.

The *grachtengordel,* the horseshoe of concentric canals that encloses the city centre, is the city's most timeless area. Names such as Prinsengracht (Princes' Canal), Herengracht (Gentlemen's Canal) and Keizersgracht (Emperor's Canal) are redolent of golden-age elegance. Work on the canals began in 1613, and the richly-gabled town houses represented the wealth that was a hallmark of the young Dutch Republic. Remnants of 17th-century life survive along this semicircle of patrician canals – in the adjacent craftsmen's community of the Jordaan; in the Dam, whose Stadhuis (town hall) was so imposing that the House of Orange turned it into a royal palace; and among the narrow canals and crooked houses of the *walletjes* (the old centre), which today constitutes the city's notorious red-light district.

While the war with Spain ebbed and flowed, fresh ideas swept through the worlds of art, architecture and science, and explorers and merchants opened up new worlds. In contrast to the landed wealth of much of the continent, Amsterdam's prosperity gave rise to a large, confident middle class, whose members were eager to appreciate the finer things in life.

Population Explosion

In the first half of the 17th century, the city's population soared from 60,000 to nearly 220,000. In addition to accepting Catholics from countries that persecuted them for their beliefs, Protestant Amsterdam welcomed Huguenot and Walloon immigrants from France, Lutherans from Germany and Jews from Germany and Portugal, thereby setting a precedent for tolerance. Moreover, numerous inhabitants of colonised territories, in Africa, the Far and Middle East and the West Indies, migrated to the city, which established a reputation as Europe's most cosmopolitan city. The resultant ethnic mix can still be seen.

Equally significant was the establishment, in 1602, of the Verenigde Oostindische Compagnie (VOC), the United East India Company, which handled trade with the Orient; its counterpart for the West Indies was founded in 1621. The Bank of Amsterdam opened its doors in 1609 and the Amsterdam Stock Exchange in 1611. The long and difficult sea journeys to the country's far-flung possessions required stout ships, and the VOC's shipyard at Oostenburg in Amsterdam became the world's largest industrial complex. Today you can see a replica East Indiaman, as the vessels were called: the *Amsterdam* is tied to a quay at the Scheepvaartmuseum (Maritime Museum),

Above: the importance of waterways, seen in a map dating back more than 450 years its tall masts a distinctive sight in the harbour. Ships such as the *Amsterdam* ploughed through the oceans, and returned laden with exotic products. One such expedition landed a hoard of late Ming Dynasty pottery, which gave birth to the Delftware (tin-glazed earthenware) industry.

The wonderful art that emerged at this time was the direct result of the wealth of the Dutch middle class. In contrast with the artists of the Italian Renaissance, who were dependent on commissions from powerful patrons, Dutch painters could sell their works to the highest bidder, who was very often an ordinary, if rich, citizen. Artists were no longer beholden to the whims and vanity of princes, popes and doges but could paint whatever took their fancy – portraits of ordinary people, still-life works and, not infrequently, the cows for which the country is still famous. Which is not to say that burghers didn't want to impress their friends by commissioning self-portraits.

Rembrandt's masterpieces

The artists of the Netherlands' golden age transformed the way we look at things. In eschewing rigid classical concepts, Frans Hals (1580–1666) founded the Dutch school of realism. A key precept of this aesthetic was to capture real, if momentary, emotions at the expense of the posed, stilted portraiture of the past. Undoubtedly the greatest artist of the period was Rembrandt van Rijn (1606–69), who was 25 when he moved from Leiden to Amsterdam. During the following four decades, Rembrandt produced a series

Above and Right: Rembrandt's *The Night Watch* and *Old Woman Reading a Lectionary*

of veritable masterpieces. His most famous painting, *The Night Watch* (1642) – which today hangs in the city's Rijksmuseum – illustrates a colourfully uniformed Amsterdam militia company. This work represents Rembrandt at the height of his considerable powers.

Neither the artists' inspiration, nor the city's golden age could last. By the 18th century, a decline, both aesthetic and commercial, was evident. Though international trade was the focal point of Dutch wealth, the country was not destined to be a long-standing colonial force in the way that Britain and France were. The Dutch were simply reluctant to put down roots in distant lands – they missed the opportunity to settle the West Indies, for instance, a failure which ultimately led to the loss of Brazil to Portugal.

The Dutch also lost out in the military and diplomatic fields. As a result of defeats by England in the mid-17th century, they lost substantial parts of

the trading empire in the East Indies. And, had England not been able to seize vital colonies in America, New York might have remained New Amsterdam. Though it was that city's Dutch governor, Peter Minuit, who made the bargain of the millennium in 'buying' Manhattan island from its Amer-ican-Indian inhabitants for the proverbial $24-worth of beads in 1626, the Dutch gave up their claims to the New Netherlands in exchange for nothing more than an English promise not to capture Dutch Guyana.

In 1795 Amsterdam was invaded by the French and in 1808 Napoleon installed his brother, Louis, as king of the Netherlands, with Amsterdam as his capital. Following Napoleon's ignominious exit from a Europe he had dominated for 20 years, the Netherlands' northern and southern provinces were united, though the latter achieved independence as Belgium in 1831. Holland did manage to retain much of its empire, the fruits of which – coffee, rubber, timber – remained vital staples of the economy until well into the 20th century.

World War I

The country sided with neither the Allied nor Axis powers in World War I, but this neutrality made little impression on the Nazis, who invaded on 10 May 1940. Prince Bernhard wanted to stay with his people in their hour of need, but his mother, Queen Wilhelmina, insisted that, in the interests of the monarchy, he accompany his wife and two daughters to Canada. By way of a compromise, Bernhard spent the war in England, where he headed the Dutch free forces. Across the Atlantic, Princess Juliana brought up the young princesses, of whom the elder, Beatrix, became queen of the Nether-lands on Juliana's abdication in 1980. In Amsterdam, meanwhile, the prince's birthday was honoured by thousands of citizens donning white carnations.

Above: in the 18th century Amsterdam was a thriving metropolis

In another, even more courageous, act of defiance, the city's dockers led a general strike in protest at the first deportation of Amsterdam's Jews. The two-day strike has gone down in Dutch history as Amsterdam's 'day beyond praise'. The most famous Dutch victim of the Holocaust was Anne Frank, whose diary is a moving testament to the life of a Jewish family in hiding. Today Anne Frank Huis is one of the city's busiest tourist sites.

The country was still recovering from the long years of Nazi occupation when disaster struck. It is only due to Dutch engineering skill that the Netherlands has kept its head above water for the past 1,000 years, but in 1953 a combination of bad weather conditions sent the North Sea crashing through the sea defences in Zeeland. More than 1,800 people lost their lives. Canals, windmills, dikes and polders all tell the story of reclamation from the sea.

In the post-war period, Amsterdam developed a reputation for social liberalism with sex, drugs and squatting in the forefront. The Dutch, especially Amsterdammers, are renowned for their tolerance. But for all its progressive – or sinful, depending on your point of view – attitudes, more innocuous traditions continue to attract enormous numbers of visitors.

Tulips from Amsterdam

Holland's love affair with tulips dates back to 1594, when the botanist Carolus Clusius first cultivated the flower at the University of Leiden. From this modest beginnings has arisen an industry of truly astonishing proportions. In the 17th century fortunes were made and lost over a single bulb. Today the Bollenstreek (bulb district) south of Amsterdam is an enormous expanse of multi-hued tulip fields, and tulip lovers pour into Holland from all over the world. Tours by bus, boat, taxi, train, bicycle, on foot and from the sky all focus on the bulb fields. The gardens at Keukenhof in particular are frequently overrun, and the song *Tulips From Amsterdam* has entered the ranks of international folk cliché.

In the art world, Amsterdam has maintained the traditions of cutting-edge excellence established by the great masters of the 17th century. The post-World War II COBRA movement (an acronym of Copenhagen, Brussels and Amsterdam) was one of the 20th century's most influential. The COBRA museum in the Amsterdam suburb of Amstelveen opened in 1995, and the COBRA Cafe on the Museumplein pays tribute to this seminal, but short-lived, group of artists. In recent decades a new generation of Dutch artists – the likes of Arnold Mik and Marijke van Warmerdam – have come into their own, and a number of galleries in the city give a good overview of the state of contemporary Dutch art.

Right: *Flowers* by Hans Bollongier

The performing arts come into their own in the summer, when Amsterdam hosts music, dance and drama festivals in parks, squares, concert halls and even on the water. The highlight of the season is the Royal Concertgebouw Orchestra's concert in the Vondelpark. In June the Holland Festival incorporates a diverse array of opera, theatre and dance productions; at the end of August the Museumplein hosts a three-day fair, featuring theatre, music and dance, in preparation for the coming cultural season. Less formally, the Leidseplein has for years hosted buskers, mime artists and fire-eaters.

The Gay Capital

If the profusion of culture and arts events in the city is responsible for the nickname the 'capital of inspiration', a relatively long-standing tolerance of homosexuality has earned it the soubriquet the 'gay capital of Europe'. There are at least 35 gay bars, plus a couple of lesbian cafes, more than a dozen predominantly gay hotels and several gay discos. The highlight of Amsterdam's gay calendar is the Gay Pride celebration that takes place on the first weekend of August.

A simple concept underlines everyday life in the city: the quest for *gezelligheid* – an enigmatic concept that is used to describe the special something that makes a place friendly, cosy and memorable. Although Amsterdam is one of Europe's great cities, it is intimate and accessible, with the ambience of a cosmopolitan village rather than a soulless metropolis. It is a city in which locals and visitors alike benefit from a glorious past while enjoying the fruits of a vibrant, tolerant present.

Above: a land of windmills
Left: traditional costume

HISTORY HIGHLIGHTS

circa 1200 Herring fishermen settle at the mouth of the River Amstel.

circa 1220 The first dam is built to hold back the tidal waters of the Zuiderzee at a settlement that becomes known as Aemstelledamme.

1275 Count Floris V exempts the people of Aemstelledamme from tolls on travel and trade.

1300 The Bishop of Utrecht grants Amsterdam its city charter.

1334 Work begins on the Oude Kerk, the city's first parish church.

1345 'Miracle of the Host' – a dying man regurgitates the Communion bread and it remains intact when thrown on a fire.

1395 The city's first town hall is built in Dam Square.

1400 Work begins on the Nieuwe Kerk.

1414 Amsterdam becomes Holland's biggest town, with a population of 12,000.

1452 Fire destroys most of the timber-built city.

1480 Defensive walls are built.

1535 Protestant Anabaptists occupy the town hall. The revolt is suppressed and Catholicism imposed.

1566 The city's first Calvinist church is established.

1576 Amsterdam, loyal to the Catholic King Philip II of Spain, is besieged by Prince William of Orange.

1578 The city surrenders and the churches and government are taken over by Calvinists.

1602 Establishment of the United East India Company, with its headquarters in Amsterdam.

1609 Bank of Amsterdam opens.

1611 Amsterdam Stock Exchange opens.

1613 Work on the *grachtengordel* – the Herengracht, Keizersgracht and Prinsengracht canals – begins.

1632 Establishment of the Athenaeum Illustre, which later became Amsterdam University.

1642 Rembrandt paints his most famous work *The Night Watch* (today exhibited in the Rijksmuseum.

1648 Work begins on new town hall.

1650 The city's population reaches 220,000.

1745 Schools for needy children are established.

1795 Amsterdam is captured by anti-monarchist Patriots and becomes the capital of the pro-French-Revolution Batavian Republic.

1806 Napoleon abolishes the republic and proclaims his brother Louis as king of the Netherlands, with Amsterdam as his capital.

1845 Pro-democracy riots lead to the establishment of a constitution.

1876 North Sea Canal opens.

1928 Amsterdam hosts the Olympic Games.

1940 Nazi Germany invades and occupies Holland.

1941 Workers, led by dockers, strike for two days in protest against the deportation of the city's Jews.

1942 Anne Frank and her family go into hiding.

1945 Amsterdam is liberated by the Allies.

1965 Anti-establishment Provos win seats on the city council.

1966 Protesters disrupt the wedding of Princess Beatrix.

1990 Van Gogh centenary exhibition.

1992 Amsterdammers vote to curb car use in the city.

1997 The Treaty of Amsterdam leads to the establishment of the euro as the common European currency.

2000 Amsterdam co-hosts the Euro 2000 football championships.

2002 The euro becomes the country's official currency.

City
Itineraries

The following itineraries consist of three full-day tours of Amsterdam's most important sights followed by a series of half-day and evening tours that explore other interesting areas and aspects of the city. After the city itineraries, three day-long, out-of-town excursions suggest visits to Haarlem and Zandvoort, the IJsselmeer and The Hague.

Most of the old city centre within the concentric circles of the golden-age canals is small and compact enough to be easily covered on foot. Amsterdammers think of the old city centre as a village. For travel beyond this neighbourhood, a combination of walking and riding on trams is highly recommended. Should you want to take a taxi, water taxi, canal bus, or the museum boat, bear in mind that all of these options are expensive. There is no better way of seeing this city of 165 canals than from one of its dozens of glass-topped canal boats. These excursions are justifiably very popular.

Hiring a car, or driving your own vehicle, is definitely not recommended. For one thing, Amsterdam has canals where other cities, Venice notwithstanding, have streets. Moreover, driving in the city has been limited since the municipality voted to stem the flow of cars some years ago. Parking is expensive, and the *dienst parkeerbeheer* (parking authority) takes its work very seriously. If you park illegally, you will invariably be caught; your car will be clamped or towed away, you will have to collect it from a car-pound out in the sticks, and then be obliged to pay a hefty fine to get it back.

Bicycles Abound

The bicycle is one of the most popular means of transport in Amsterdam – the city's 500,000 cyclists take advantage of the remarkably flat terrain. There are lots of places from which to hire a bike, and any number of bike lanes. Drawbacks to look out for include tram tracks – cross them at right angles to avoid getting your wheels caught; heavy traffic – locals think nothing of driving through red lights or on the tram tracks; and the potential for having your bike stolen – be sure to lock it whenever you leave it unattended.

Whatever your mode of transport, don't hesitate to venture off the beaten track and make your own discoveries. One delight of exploring Amsterdam is stumbling upon idiosyncratic details. These could be an unusually-shaped gable, an offbeat little store, a gaily-painted bicycle, or a sunken canal boat. Another attraction of this sophisticated city is the friendliness of its people, and the high level of English spoken, so don't be shy of striking up a conversation with strangers. This is a city that makes visitors welcome without even trying.

Left: café on the bank of the Singel canal
Right: one of the city's ornate gables

Central Amsterdam

200 m / 220 yds

---- Itinerary 1
---- Itinerary 2

JORDAAN

CENTRUM

CENTRAAL STATION

1. THE GOLDEN-AGE CANALS *(see map, p22)*

This day-long itinerary follows the concentric semi-circle of 16th- and 17th-century canals – the Singel, Herengracht, Keizersgracht and Prinsengracht. Highlights include Anne Frank Huis, several museums and some offbeat stores. A substantial amount of walking is involved but there are lots of 'time out' possibilities along the way.

Begin west of Centraal Station at the junction of Haarlemmer Houttuinen and Korte Prinsengracht. If you are arriving from Centraal Station, you will find it easier to walk to the starting point, along Prins Hendrikkade to Haarlemmer Houttuinen, than to take public transport.

The canals around which this itinerary is based are lasting testimony to the country's golden age. It is unfortunate that the glories of that heyday have been tarnished by the industrial by-products associated with the 20th century – noise, pollution, parking problems and the dog excrement that litters the parks and pavements – but these minor annoyances do not detract from the wonders of a city that was once one of the fonts of western civilisation.

Starting at the Korte Prinsengracht–Haarlemmer Houttuinen junction, walk along the narrow canal to the corner of **Brouwersgracht** (Brewers' Canal) and **Prinsengracht**. Note how all of the former brewery warehouses have been converted into expensive apartments along Brouwersgracht. At the junction of the two canals are a couple of recommended spots, should you

fancy a breakfast snack: **Café Tabac**, (101 Brouwersgracht) and the oddly named brown cafe **'t Papeneiland** at 2 Prinsengracht. Brown cafés (*bruine kroegen*) are old, traditional-style Dutch bars known for their colour, which comes from the wood being stained by centuries of smoke.

Market Square

Cross Brouwersgracht by the bridge here, then switch to the west (right) bank of Prinsengracht. The first stop is **Noordermarkt** and the **Noorderkerk** (North Church) that stands in the market square. On Saturday Noordermarkt hosts a **Bird Market** and, selling organically-grown produce, a **Farmers' Market**. On Monday morning there's a textiles and a second-hand market here. Some gables overlooking the square feature agricultural images – of cows, chickens and the like – that recall the square's historical role as a market. The Noorderkerk, designed by Hendrick de Keyser, the golden-age's master church builder, dates to 1623.

Continue along Prinsengracht to the bridge at Prinsenstraat, and turn left along this short street, which is lined with cafés and restaurants. Cross over the **Keizersgracht** bridge – note the houseboats moored on either side – onto Heerenstraat and continue to **Herengracht** before turning right along the canal. Continue to the **Theatermuseum** (168 Herengracht; Tues–Fri 11am–5pm, Sat and Sun 1–5pm; entrance fee). The museum occupies five

Right: all set for a pleasant canal cruise

adjacent canal houses, one of which, the **Bartolotti House** at No. 166, was built around 1618 by Pieter de Keyser, son of the great church architect Hendrick de Keyser, and is famous for its red-brick gable. In the museum you will find a wide variety of costumes, maquettes, masks, puppets, photographs, paintings and stage backdrops, covering all forms of theatre.

Anne Frank's House

Backtrack a few steps to Leliegracht, go up onto Prinsengracht and turn left to visit the **Anne Frank Huis** (263 Prinsengracht; Apr–Aug: daily 9am–9pm; Sept–Mar: daily 9am–7pm; tel: 556 7100; entrance fee). The earlier you arrive at Anne Frank Huis the better, because the queues do sometimes become very long. In summer especially you might have to wait in line for an hour or more. This is the house in which the teenage Jewish diarist, Anne Frank (1929–45) hid with her family (and two other families) for more than two years during World War II before being captured by the

Nazis, at whose hands she died of hunger and disease in Bergen-Belsen concentration camp. This is one of Amsterdam's most popular 'attractions'.

Most people consider the wait worthwhile. Not that there is much to see inside: that's the whole point. The rooms in which the Franks hid are as bare as they were on the day the family was betrayed and taken to the death camp. But it is not difficult, using your imagination and powers of empathy, to put yourself in Anne's situation, awakening as a young woman, and telling her secret thoughts to the diary. Her life was extinguished; her spirit lives on.

The Anne Frank Huis might leave you feeling somewhat sombre, if not depressed. If so, or if you need a break for lunch or a drink anyway, try the **Rum Runners** at 277 Prinsengracht. This Caribbean-

Above: Prinsengracht houseboats
Left: Anne Frank Huis

style cafe-restaurant does an excellent guacamole and wonderful margaritas, along with a variety of other sunnily-disposed dishes and drinks. One of four **Canal Bikes** moorings is on Prinsengracht outside Rum Runners. You might want to spend an hour pottering about on the water at this point (but for a separate tour, see *Itinerary 7, The Canals by Canal Bike, page 42*).

Continue a few steps to **Westermarkt** and the **Westerkerk** (Mon–Sat 11am–3pm), a Renaissance-style church built between 1620 and 1631. The latter date marked the opening of its tower, the **Westertoren** (guided tours Jun–Sept: daily 10am–6pm; entrance fee), which is surmounted by the blue, red and gold crown of the Holy Roman Empire, a symbol bestowed by the Austrian Emperor Maximilian. The church is where you will find Rembrandt's tomb. Also on Westermarkt is a sculpture of Anne Frank and the marble triangle of the **Homomonument**, dedicated to the gay and lesbian victims of homophobic persecution down the centuries.

Across the street at 33 Westermarkt, on the corner of Prinsengracht, is another lunch option, the **Kalkhoven**, a traditional old brown café with rugs on the tables and hard drinkers around the bar. Before continuing along Prinsengracht, you might want to make a short diversion, to the right, to 17 Rozengracht, to visit the **Blue Gold Fish**, an intriguingly offbeat jewellery-cum-gift shop with a style all its own.

Eight Thousand Buttons

Continue along Prinsengracht, past the Pulitzer Hotel, to Reestraat. At No. 8 is the Pulitzer's up-market restaurant **De Goudsbloem**, and at No. 4 the **Café Pulitzer**. At Keizersgracht turn right and continue as far as Wolvenstraat, where the **Knopen Winkel** (Button Shop) at No. 16 stocks some 8,000 different varieties of button – just in case you might have lost one recently. At Herengracht go right to Wijde Heisteeg, then head back once again to the Singel Canal and on to the square called Spui. This square is quite fascinating, and is a major constituent of the next itinerary (see *Itinerary 2, The Principal Squares, page 28*). You might however want to adjourn for a coffee break here at **Café Hoppe** (18–20 Spuistraat), another traditional brown café, or at the chic **Grand-Café Luxembourg** (24 Spuistraat).

Either way, walk alongside the far bank of Singel to the **Bloemenmarkt** (Floating Flower Market), which is one of Amsterdam's most special sites. It's like a botanical garden set adrift on the canal, with heaps of flowers changing hands. This is probably the best – and is certainly the most atmospheric – place at which to buy cut flowers and bulbs. You are now at **Muntplein**, a busy tram intersection, and its **Munttoren** (Mint Tower). The base of the tower used to be part of the Reguliers Gate in the city wall, and in 1620 Hendrick de Keyser added the ornate, lead-covered bell tower whose bells sing out gaily every Tuesday and Friday at 12.30pm and 1pm respectively.

Turn right along Vijzelstraat to Herengracht to visit the **Kattenkabinet** (Cat Museum, 497 Herengracht; open

Right: the steeple of the 17th-century Westerkerk

– when there is an exhibition – Mon–Fri 11am–2pm and 1–5pm, Sat and Sun 1–5pm; entrance fee). This museum is dedicated to depictions of our feline friends. Sculptures, paintings and prints show the role of the cat in art and culture through the centuries. The golden-age merchants' houses ranged along the bend in the canal at this point give rise to this neighbourhood's name: the Golden Bend.

Patrician residences

Proceed up Vijzelstraat to Keizersgracht and turn left to visit the **Museum van Loon** (672 Keizersgracht; Fri–Mon 11am–5pm; entrance fee). This museum gives you a glimpse behind the gables at what a patrician house – in this case a double house dating from 1672 – of the era immediately following the golden age would have looked like. Its restored period rooms are filled with richly decorated panelling, stucco work, mirrors, fireplaces, furnishings, porcelain, medallions, chandeliers, rugs, and so forth. The marble staircase, complete with intricately designed balustrade, is itself a masterpiece.

Continue across Reguliersgracht to Utrechtsestraat, a fascinating shopping street with some good restaurants, such as the Indonesian **Tempo Doeloe** at No. 75. To see another richly-decorated, 17th-century patrician canal house, head north to the junction with Herengracht and turn right to the **Willet-Holthuysen Museum** (605 Herengracht; Mon–Fri 10am–5pm, Sat and Sun 11am–5pm; entrance fee). Check out the dining salon, with a table set under the chandelier for what looks like a pretty fancy meal.

A walk to the end of Herengracht is rewarded by a picturesque scene at the **River Amstel**. If you want to treat yourself, have dinner at the superb, continental-style restaurant **Moko** (12 Amstelveld; Wed, Thur, Sun, Mon 11.30am–1am, Fri, Sat 11.30am–2am; tel: 020-626 1199), which on warm summer evenings spreads an open-air terrace onto the tree-shaded square.

2. THE PRINCIPAL SQUARES *(see map, p22)*

Visit the city's main squares on this full-day tour. Highlights include the tranquil Spui, with its great second-hand book stalls, glitzy Rembrandtplein, the popular Kalverstraat shopping area and the Spiegelkwartier antiques district. End the day at the wild and wonderful Leidseplein. This itinerary involves a lot of walking, but there are countless tempting cafes for breaks.

Start at the Dam, which can be reached by taking any of the following trams: 1, 2, 4, 5, 9, 13, 14, 16, 17, 20, 24 and 25 from Centraal Station.

The **Dam**, which isn't a dam any more, marks the spot where the first dam was built on the River Amstel in the 13th century, an event that led to the establishment of the city. Now it is Amsterdam's most monumental square. Before you set out from the Dam, you might want to take breakfast at the elegant **Grand Hotel Krasnapolsky** (9 Dam). If so, it's well worth taking a turn around the ground floor of the hotel, which was opened in 1866 by a former Polish tailor; the restored Wintertuin (Winter Garden) restaurant is an extravagant example of Victorian-era aesthetics.

Beside the hotel is Amsterdam's premier department store, the **Bijenkorf** (1 Dam), to which you might want to return at a later date. Also on this side of the square is the insipid (or understated, if you like this sort of thing) **Nationaal Monument**, a 22-metre (72-ft) high obelisk commemorating Holland's liberation from German occupation in World War II. Cross the road that bisects the Dam, to the **Koninklijk Paleis** (Royal Palace; Tues–Thur 1–4pm, around Easter and in summer: daily 12.30–5pm; entrance fee). Constructed by Jacob van Campen between 1648 and 1655, the building served as the town hall, until Napoleon Bonaparte's lesser-known younger brother Louis was appointed king of the Netherlands and took it for his palace in 1808. The Royal Palace compensates for its rather heavy-handed neo-classical exterior with an elegant interior that brims with white marble.

Church of Coronations

More interesting might be an exhibition at the neo-Gothic **Nieuwe Kerk** (New Church), the Netherlands' coronation church which, when monarchs are not being crowned, is mostly used as an exhibition space and recital venue (it has two superb 16th- and 17th-century organs). Famous Dutch military figures such as the 17th-century hero Michiel de Ruyter, as well as the poet Vondel, are buried here. The final point of interest in the Dam neighbourhood is **Madame Tussaud's** (20 Dam; Sept–Jun: daily 10am–5.30pm; Jul and Aug: daily 9.30am–5.30pm; entrance fee). Featured among the waxworks museum's models are Dutch personalities such as Rembrandt and Mata Hari, and a cast of international big names such as Churchill and Gandhi.

Above Left: relaxing in a cafe. **Left:** the Amstel skyline, illuminated at dusk
Right: the monumental Dam square marks the spot where the city was founded

The Historical Museum

For some more background history, head along Kalverstraat, Amsterdam's popular pedestrians-only shopping street, to the **Amsterdams Historisch Museum** (Historical Museum, 92 Kalverstraator and 357 Nieuwezijds Voorburgwal; Mon–Fri 10am–5pm, Sat and Sun 11am–5pm; entrance fee). The museum takes visitors on a trip through the centuries, illustrating Amsterdam's transformation from a muddy medieval fishing village, through the expansive sea power of the golden age, to today's sophisticated metropo-

lis. The museum is housed in a 16th-century orphanage.

If you are ready for lunch at this point, leave through the museum's Nieuwezijds Voorburgwal exit, walk a short distance to Spui square then take a right into **Spuistraat**. Here, at No. 24, you will notice the **Grand-Café Luxembourg**. Although a tad pretentious in some people's opinion, it serves good food – many of its dishes are specialities taken from the menus of well-regarded restaurants and cafés in the city. Alternatively you could try **Hoppe** (No 18–20), a brown cafe popular with students and journalists.

Browsing through Books

After lunch you should be ready for **Spui**. On one corner you will find the **Athenaeum News and Book Centre**, which has a good range of international titles. Outside is *'t Lievertje* (Little Darling), a bronze sculpture of a boy standing with hands on hips and grinning broadly at passers-by. Every Friday there is a good second-hand book market in Spui (and a Sunday art market from March to September). Waterstone's, the British bookshop chain, has a branch on the square, although the entrance is at 152 Kalverstraat. Also superb for books is the **American Book Center**, a short way along Kalverstraat at No 185: it's open most days till 8pm, on Thursday till 10pm.

If you walk down Spui to No. 10–17, you will reach the **Begijnhof**. This beautiful, tranquil courtyard dates from 1346 and for centuries was the home of pious, unmarried Catholic laywomen – *begijns*, who lived a semi-monastic life in the service of the community. The last *begijn* died in 1970. The Begijnhof's little gabled houses, built between the 14th and 17th centuries are now the homes of elderly retired women – try not to disturb them. In spring the Begijnhof's lawn's carpet of daffodils and crocuses complements the spiritual atmosphere. The Begijnhof's 17th-century Presbyterian church was originally Catholic – the *begijns* were compelled to hand it over after the triumph of Calvinism in Amsterdam. Further along, **Het Houten Huys** (The Wooden House) at No. 34 dates from 1460. It is the city's oldest house and one of only two remaining wooden residences (for the other one, see *Itinerary 4, The Old Centre, page 37*).

Walk along Spui to **Rokin**, where you will see the canal-boat moorings of the Rederij P Kooij ferry company. Here too is the traditional cigar-and-pipe shop **P G C Hajenius** (Nos 92–96), whose humidors are world-renowned. Continue along Rokin to Muntplein (see *Itinerary 1, The Golden Age Canals, page 25*), then across to Reguliersbreestraat. At a later date you might want to take in a movie at the startlingly Art Deco **Tuschinski Theater** at Nos 26–28; in the meantime, take a turn around its magnificent lobby.

If you didn't have lunch, try a felafel at **Falafel Koning** in Reguliersteeg, opposite the Tuschinski – take it away to eat over a great view: the bridge over the Binnenamstel, at the point where the River Amstel runs into the city and the maze of canals. Continue into **Rembrandtplein** and check out an undistinguished statue of Rembrandt in the little garden at its centre. Busy, brassy Rembrandtplein is full of mediocre-to-average cafes, where aspiring musicians play in the evening. If you're looking for quality, try the **Royal Café De Kroon** at No. 17, which has a lovely enclosed balcony that overlooks the square; alternatively, at No. 26–36 is **Café Schiller** – the wood-panelled bar of the Hotel Schiller. (For further options, see *Itinerary 14: Rembrandtplein, page 54*.)

Art and Antiques

Leave the square by Thorbeckeplein. If you're passing this way on a Sunday afternoon (between March and December), you will pass through the street stalls of the **Thorbeckeplein Art Market**, a sophisticated little gathering that sits somewhat incongruously beside the topless bars in this small, handsome square. Then take Herengracht, Vijzelstraat and Keizersgracht. There isn't a good way to do this by public transport, and you must at least partially retrace a section of *Itinerary 1: The Golden Age Canals (see page 23)* to Nieuwe Spiegelstraat and its extension along Spiegelgracht. You are now in the **Spiegelkwartier** antiques district, where antiques shops are thickly clustered along the narrow street and the pretty canal. Look out for the wonderfully old-fashioned toy shop,

Above Left: gable stone at the Historical Museum. **Left:** the Hoppe brown café
Right: the Little Darling sculpture outside the Athenaeum News and Book Centre

the **Bell Tree**, at 10 Spiegelgracht. Not only do none of the toys bleep, whirr or zap, but a good many are actually made of wood.

Emerging from the antiques district into **Kleine Lijnbaansgracht**, turn right past a higgledy-piggledy row of canal houses, and a parade of restaurants, to **Leidseplein**. In the summer this district comes into its own as a centre of entertainment. In addition to the cafes, restaurants, theatres, cinemas and clubs, there is any number of diverse street performers, typically fire-eaters and buskers *(see Itinerary 13: Leidseplein, page 52)*. As you stroll around the square, soaking up the atmosphere, remember to be wary of pickpockets.

Cafés for People-watching

Leidseplein's cafes are good for people-watching. Particularly recommended is **Reijnders** at No. 6: it retains elements of old-world, brown-café charm, and it has a cosy terrace. A good choice for afternoon tea is the Café Américain in the American Hotel at 97 Leidsekade. The building is a good example of the *jugendstil* architectural style. This, the German answer to Art Nouveau, means 'young style', and is a recurring motif of the city's landscape. Check out which movies are showing at the many cinemas around the square.

Although by now it will be quite late in the day, there may still be people

playing chess with huge plastic pieces at **Max Euweplein**, a satellite of Leidseplein. Here, too, is the **Holland Casino Amsterdam** and the mooring of Rederij Noord-Zuid, a canal-boat company.

Among the enormous choice of eateries in this neighbourhood, you could opt to dine at the excellent seafood restaurant, **De Oesterbar**, at 10 Leidseplein, or **Alfonso's**, a Mexican restaurant just off the square at 69 Korte Leidsedwarsstraat. After that, if you're still wide awake and suitably dressed, you may want to try your luck at the casino on Max Euweplein.

Above: the Begijnhof at Spui 10–17
Left: a fine model in the antiques district

3. THE MUSEUM QUARTER *(see map, p32)*

This itinerary focuses on the city's most important museums: the **Rijksmuseum, Van Gogh Museum,** and **Stedelijk Museum.** If three museums is too much for one day, skip the Rijksmuseum or the Stedelijk but don't miss the Van Gogh. The route also takes in the Concertgebouw concert hall, two of the city's premier shopping streets and Vondelpark.

Start on Stadhouderskade at the entrance to the Rijksmuseum, one stop east of Leidseplein by No. 6, 7 or 10 tram. Wear comfortable walking shoes.

The museums of Amsterdam are so outstanding that, even if it happens to be a beautiful day, you might choose to sacrifice the sunshine for some high culture. Such is their quality, these galleries have been known to tranform apathetic philistines into passionate aesthetes; even if you know nothing of art, you will probably appreciate the offerings withing their august walls.

Straight ahead is the **Rijksmuseum** (State Museum, 42 Stadhouderskade; daily 10am–5pm; tel: 673 2121; entrance fee), whose collection of Dutch and Flemish paintings from the 15th to the 18th centuries is the finest in the world. The gigantic neo-Gothic building, designed by P.J.H Cuypers, first opened is doors in 1885, when it exhibited a collection from The Hague's National Art Gallery that had been brought to Amsterdam in 1808 by King Louis Napoleon. The Rijksmuseum is very big and somewhat bewildering so, for more than a quick view of the highlights, you might want to return at a later date. But for this single-morning dash, it's a good idea to arrive by 10am and stay until you're ready for lunch.

The Night Watch

To start with the foremost attraction, follow the arrows upstairs to the end of the first floor, where you will find Rembrandt's *The Night Watch*. Painted in 1642, this group portrait of a colourfully attired militia company has come to represent not only Rembrandt but the entire Dutch golden age. Its iconic status might not be immediately apparent – don't be surprised if, like many visitors, you are far from overwhelmed at first sight. The militiamen themselves hated the picture and their hostile reception sent Rembrandt into a tailspin that led to bankruptcy: a classic case of the prophet not being honoured in his own land. Yet it is a magnificent spectacle when viewed as a whole, a *tour de force* of colour, light and composition. Up close you can focus on the individual faces (including Rembrandt's own visage), which express the confidence and pride of a young nation that had liberated itself from the Spanish colonial yoke and saw an exciting new world opening up before it. Be prepared for some queuing if you want to see the work from a good vantage point.

A host of other great paintings by the Dutch masters hang on nearby walls, each in glorious isolation – portraits by Frans Hals and Vermeer,

Above: a pensive cherub at the Rijksmuseum

city itineraries

landscapes by Jacob van Ruisdael, bawdy escapades by Jan Steen, and any number of others. In addition to the painting department the museum has four major subdivisions: Dutch History, Prints, Sculpture and Decorative Arts, and Asian Art, covering 150 rooms in total. A superb display of model ships includes intricately rigged sailing ships, and there are collections of doll's houses, furniture, clocks, Delft blue porcelain and masses of other pieces from 1,000 years of Dutch history.

A Worthy Plaza

Leave the Rijksmuseum on Museumstraat, which cuts across **Museumplein**. This big square has been redeveloped from a chaotic tour-bus parking lot to a plaza worthy of the cultural institutions that surround it. The tour buses and other traffic have gone underground, literally, and the old Museumstraat has been replaced by a garden with a long pool on which people ice-skate in the winter. The new tranquility is augmented by the presence of a café-restaurant and a food store.

Walk through the park to the end of Museumplein, to **Van Baerlestraat** and the **Concertgebouw** (Concert Building, 2–6 Concertgebouwplein). Built in 1887 by the architect A.L. van Gendt, this is one of the world's great classical music halls and the home of the Concertgebouw Orchestra.

A golden lyre stands on the roof above the entrance, and the neo-classical colonnade is watched over by severe portrait busts of Beethoven, Sweelinck and Bach. Among the composers who have held court here are Brahms, Stravinsky, Strauss and Mahler. If you are here on a Wednesday around lunchtime, you may be able to listen to the orchestra rehearsing for free. Or you might want to buy tickets for an evening concert.

There is an excellent restaurant next door to the Concertgebouw, **Bodega Keyzer** (96 Van Baerlestraat), where, in a much recounted incident, a musician from the Concertgebouw Orchestra was once mistaken for a waiter. Or you could walk south along Van Baerlestraat to **De Knijp** at No. 134, which is equally good and less stuffy. For what might be the best option of all, walk a little further, to Roelof Hartplein, for lunch in the chic café-restaurant **De Wildschuut**, which has a pavement terrace, at Nos 1–3.

Modern Art

After lunch, retrace your steps along Van Baerlestraat, passing the Concertgebouw, to the **Stedelijk Museum** (13 Paulus Potterstraat; daily 11am–5pm; tel: 573 2737; entrance fee). Built in neo-Renaissance style in 1895, with funds bequeathed by an elderly widow and art lover, the Stedelijk (which means Municipal) stretches the definition of modern art back to the mid-19th century, winding up at the end of the 20th century. It has an amazing collection of non-Dutch masters, including works by Braque, Breitner, Calder, Cézanne, Chagall, Israëls, Kandinsky, Malevich, Manet, Matisse, Monet, Oldenburg, Picasso, Renoir, Rosenquist and Warhol.

The Dutch collection is outstanding, particularly the Appel collection. There are De Koonings and Mondrians here, though if you want to see the country's biggest collection of Mondrians (together with a few works by Van Gogh) you will have to visit the Haags Gemeentemuseum in The Hague. The Stedelijk's sculpture garden features works by Moore (*Reclining Man*), Wouters (*Domestic Cares*), Couzijn (*Awakening of Africa*) and Volten (*Kubus*). A new wing is due to be added to the Stedelijk as part of the Museumplein redevelopment.

Don't be surprised if the last of the big three museums, the **Van Gogh Museum** (7 Paulus Potterstraat; daily 10am–5pm; tel: 570 5200; entrance fee) constitutes the highlight of your visit to Amsterdam. Vincent Van Gogh (1853–90) is the subject of passionate devotion throughout the world, and his paintings command astronomical prices at auction. This is particularly ironic when one thinks of the poverty and lack of recognition suffered by the artist in his short lifetime. The museum contains some 200 Van Gogh paintings – including *The Potato Eaters* and *Sunflowers*

Above Left: doll's house at the Rijksmuseum
Right: self-portrait at the Van Gogh Museum

– and 500 of his drawings, along with the artist's collection of Japanese wood carvings. The library of letters features examples of the correspondence between Vincent and his brother Theo (whose relationship formed the subject of Robert Altman's 1990 movie *Vincent & Theo*, starring Tim Roth). The museum also displays works by Toulouse-Lautrec, Gauguin and other major international artists.

Van Gogh's paintings are arranged in simple chronological order, which makes it easy to trace his development as an artist from the darkly foreboding works of his early Dutch and Belgian period, through the burgeoning of colour in Paris, to the luminous, swirling masterpieces he painted in the clear light of Provence. There is an inevitable question mark at the end of this sequence: what more would he have achieved and what recognition might he have received if he had not cut short his own life at the age of 37? Temporary exhibitions are displayed at the new, ellipse-shaped, partially subterranean wing designed by the Japanese architect Kisho Kurokawa.

Designer Clothes

Having had your fill of museums you might be in the mood for some shopping in Van Baerlestraat and the adjoining **Pieter Cornelisz Hooftstraat** (which is generally shortened to PC Hooftstraat, or 'the PC Hooft'), two blocks down Van Baerlestraat from the Stedelijk Museum. These are Amsterdam's two top-rated shopping streets and it makes sense to take advantage of being in the area. Lots of smart and trendy designer-clothes outlets are located here, particularly in the PC Hooft. Stores to look out for include, for men: **Didato** (94a PC Hooftstraat), **Questo** (126 PC Hooftstraat), and **Spirito Sportivo** (8 Van Baerlestraat); for women: **Comma** (44 PC Hooftstraat), **Laurèl** (98 PC Hooftstraat), and **Marccain** (84 PC Hooftstraat) **Focke & Meltzer**, at 65–67 P C Hooftstraat, is the best place in Amsterdam to purchase Delftware and Makkumware porcelain.

On long summer evenings, you could take in the city's atmosphere by walking to the western end of PC Hooftstraat for a leisurely stroll in **Vondelpark**, named after the poet Joost van

Above: shopping at the PC Hooft
Left: statue of the poet in Vondelpark

den Vondel. (After dark this is not such a great option because the park becomes less attractive and less safe.) The park serves as both garden and playground. In typical Dutch fashion, Vondelpark has lots of water, in the shape of long, sinuous pools around which crowds gather to sunbathe in summer. In addition to the park's usual activities – walking, cycling, jogging, frisbee-throwing, and ice-cream guzzling – one of the most enjoyable pursuits, for the young at heart at least, is roller-blading. Rent a pair of roller-blades (and protective gear) from **Duosport Rent-a-Skate** at the Amstelveenseweg end of the park and, kitted out like an imperial stormtrooper from *Star Wars*, you can power-blade (or power-stumble) around the expanses of Vondelpark.

If it's a warm evening, dine al fresco on the terrace of the Vondelpark's own **Café Vertigo**. Should something more sophisticated appeal to you, you could return to Van Baerlestraat and the **Bodega Keyzer** – be sure to order your meal from a waiter and not from the lead violin! – or to De Knijp.

4. THE OLD CENTRE (THE WALLETJES)   *(see map, p36)*

Take a leisurely stroll through the infamous Rosse Buurt (red-light district) in daylight hours, when you can appreciate the many non-erotic attractions of this beautiful old part of Amsterdam.

Start at the Dam outside the Grand Hotel Krasnapolsky, or inside if you want breakfast at the coffee bar. Allow three hours for this itinerary.

Walk along Damrak in the direction of Centraal Station, and turn right into Beursplein. Here, in addition to the fountain and tree-shaded benches, you will find the early-20th-century **Beurs van Berlage** (277 Damrak; Mon–Fri 9am–5pm; entrance fee). This, the old Stock Exchange, is now a museum, exhibition hall and concert venue. In its main hall you can admire the plain ironwork, narrow arcades, and Romanesque and neo-Renaissance motifs.

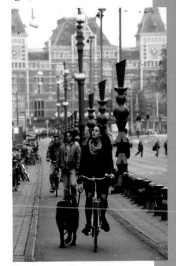

Take Beursstraat, then turn right onto Paternostersteeg, and continue through Wijde Kerksteeg to Oudekerksplein. (If by chance Paternostersteeg is closed, continue to Oude Brugsteeg, turn right into Warmoesstraat, and left into Wijde Kerksteeg for Oudekerksplein.) The foundations of the **Oude Kerk** (Old Church; Mon–Sat 11am–5pm, Sun 1–5pm; entrance fee) were laid in 1300, but the triple-naved church was not completed until 1577. A turn around the tree-shaded square gives a good impression of the red-light district: the venerable old church, pretty canal and gabled houses now seem a bit incongruous amid the prostitutes' parlours and sex clubs.

Walk along the **Oudezijds Voorburgwal** canal, past more red-fringed rooms and a couple of good second-hand bookshops. The 17th- and 18th-

Above: cycling in Damrak

century houses at Nos 101–7, 133–5, and 232 have interestingly-shaped gables. Across Damstraat, still on Oudezijds Voorburgwal, the character of the area changes to one of handsome houses and offices in the old gabled canal-side buildings. At No. 197 is **The Grand**, one of Amsterdam's swankiest hotels, located in a 16th-century building that was once the **Prinsenhof** (Royal Inn); it's well worth entering for a look. At No. 231 the **Athenaeum Illustre**, dating from 1632, was the forerunner of the University of Amsterdam, whose campus you are now entering.

Turn left into Grimburgwal, noting the scenic junction of several canals at this point. Walk to the far side of Oudezijds Achterburgwal, then right into Oudemanhuispoort, an arcade that hosts an excellent second-hand book market. Midway along the arcade, on the left, automatic doors open onto a garden courtyard. Turning left at the end of the arcade, you enter Kloveniersburgwal, passing **OostIndisch Huis** (East India House), which was once the headquarters of the United East India Company and which now houses university offices. Its main entrance is on **Oude Hoogstraat**, leading back to Oudezijds Achterburgwal.

Marijuana Museum

On the far side of the canal are three museums that bring a touch of what you might call culture (if

Above: the Oude Kerk

you're willing to stretch the term) to the red-light district. First up is the **Hash Marijuana Hemp Museum** (148 Oudezijds Achterburgwal; daily 10am–5.30pm; entrance fee). This is an educational experience. Amsterdam and the noxious weed are all but synonymous; here you get the lowdown on the high. Next comes the **Tattoo Museum** (130 Oudezijds Achterburgwal; summer: daily noon–6pm; winter: Tues–Sun noon–6pm; entrance fee), which does a similar job for the art of body decoration, with tattooing traditions from around the world. Finally there is the **Erotic Museum** (54 Oudezijds Achterburgwal; daily noon–midnight; entrance fee), which is more about decorations of a bawdy nature. It treats its subject matter seriously, and includes 19th-century photographs showing Victorians being far from prim and proper.

Cross the canal bridge and return along the canal for a short distance to Bloedstraat, then into **Nieuwmarkt**. The 14th-century **De Waag** on the square was one of the city's fortified gates. Now it is a multimedia centre with a wonderful, atmospheric restaurant. Nearby is Zeedijk, which was once a 'shooting gallery' for Amsterdam's heroin addicts. Now cleaned up, it is a fairly attractive shopping street that curves into a restaurants-and-bars zone before ending opposite Centraal Station. At No. 1 is **'t Aepje**, a wooden house dating from 1550, one of only two such houses left in the city (for the other one, see *Itinerary 2, The Principal Squares, page 29*).

5. THE ZOO DISTRICT   *(see pull-out map)*

A half-day trip to Botanical Gardens, Artis Zoo, and Tropical Museum.

Start at Waterlooplein, served by tram lines 9, 14 and 20, as well as by the metro, and sneltram lines 51, 53 and 54 to Waterlooplein metro station.

Either walk across Mr Visserplein to Muiderstraat, or hop on No. 9, 14 or 20 tram for one stop. (We revisit Waterlooplein in *Itinerary 11: The Jewish Quarter, page 48*, so you may not want to linger there now.) Cross the bridge over Nieuwe Herengracht and you will see the **Hortus Botanicus** (Botanical Garden, 2a Plantage Middenlaan; Apr–Sept: Mon–Fri 9am–5pm, Sat and Sun 11am–5pm; Oct–Mar closes at 4pm; entrance fee) on your right.

Founded in 1638 as the Hortus Medicus, the Botanical Garden is one of the world's oldest. It moved to its present location in 1682. With some 250,000 flowers and 115,000 plants and trees, including 8,000 different varieties, the garden is a medley of colour and scent, and a relaxing place for a stroll. It owes much to the treasure trove of tropical plants the Dutch found in their former colonies of Indonesia, Surinam and the Antilles, and not a little of its popularity to the national infatuation with flowers – not only tulips.

Among the garden's highlights are the **Semicircle** behind the entrance – a reconstruction of part of the original layout from 1682; the **Mexico-California**

Right: hands-on activity at the zoo

Desert House; the **Palm House**, comprising one of the world's oldest collection of palm trees; and the **Tri-Climate House**, grouping tropical, subtropical and desert plants. Opened in 1993, it features a gallery that simulates the atmosphere of a jungle. You can get a snack from the **Oranjerie** (built in 1870), or you might want to check out the shop's souvenirs.

Walk or take tram Nos. 9, 14 or 20 one stop along Plantage Middenlaan to **Artis Zoo** (38–40 Plantage Kerklaan; daily 9am–5pm; entrance fee) – the country's oldest. Like zoos throughout the world, Artis has made a big effort to replace the cruel exploitation of animals with a facility that promotes the appreciation and preservation of the natural world's living creatures, with a particular emphasis placed on authenticity. On the other hand Artis, which has been open since 1838, does still reflect the Victorian sensibility of its founders and the animals don't have much space. Either way, it's an enormous attraction, particularly for children.

The range of animals includes tigers, leopards, elephants, camels, polar bears, gorillas, peacocks, seals and so forth. There is in addition an aviary, a reptile house, a nocturnal house, a **Planetarium** (closed Mon am) and a **Geological Museum**. The zoo's garden layout and range of tree and plant species rival those of the Hortus Botanicus. The **Aquarium** is well presented, particularly the sections on the River Amazon, coral reefs, and Ams-

terdam's own canals, with their fish populations and urban detritus. Rest with a snack or lunch at the self-service **De Twee Cheetahs Restaurant**, which features a 'kiddies' corner'.

A massive expansion programme began in 1998. Phase 1, the African Savannah project, consists of a microplain that is home to zebras, wildebeest, ostriches and other birds. Phase 2, which opened in 2001, includes a play-island for children in front of the restaurant.

Continue along Plantage Middenlaan, either on foot or for two stops on the 9, 14 or 20 tram, to the **Tropenmuseum** (Tropical Museum, 2 Linnaeusstraat; daily 10am–5pm; entrance fee). As at the Hortus Botanicus, the impetus behind the Tropenmuseum came from the Dutch colonies in the tropics. The extravagant building says a lot about the European end of the colonial ideal. This is not to suggest that the museum is a dusty monument to vanished glory; it is a highly relevant evocation of life and environment in the tropics, with emphasis on the threats posed by burgeoning populations and ecological destruction. If you are travelling with youngsters, you could take them to the **Kindermuseum**, within the Tropenmuseum. It is designed for children, though of course adults are allowed, so long as they are in the guise of chaperones.

Once you have had your fill of flora and fauna, you can take the No. 9, 14 or 20 tram back to Waterlooplein.

Above: a lioness extends a loud welcome to the zoo

6. THE HARBOUR   *(see map, p40)*

Allow four hours for a tour of the old harbour. The itinerary covers the 'little islands' at one end and the Maritime Museum at the other, and includes a two-minute 'cruise' on the IJ ferry to Amsterdam North.

Start at Centraal Station. As you will be using public transport for part of the itinerary, make sure you have a strippenkaart *(strip ticket), or buy one from the bus driver* (see Practical Information: Getting Around, page 83).

It's well worth taking the time to have a good look at **Centraal Station**. Constructed on an artificial island in the IJ channel, the station opened in 1895 and, as is the fate of so much architecture, it was heartily disliked at the time. Today the station is a tourist attraction in its own right, partly for its extravagant architecture and partly for the lively atmosphere that surrounds it. Street musicians, particularly traditional barrel-organ grinders, for some reason, line up to perform here. Ten of the city's 16 tram routes begin and end their journeys at Centraal Station, as do a fair number of bus routes.

Bicycles galore

Here is a terminal for taxis, water taxis, canal buses, cruise boats and ferries. You will also find the Museumboot (Museum Boat) in the station area. Enough bicycles are chained up around here to constitute an obstacle to pedestrian navigation. Two vvv (local tourism) centres dispense information and book hotel rooms for tourists. Beware of pickpockets, here even more than elsewhere in the city. If you haven't had breakfast or you want a coffee, the **1e Klas** buffet on platform one is excellent.

Now it is time to hit the water. For a good view of Amsterdam harbour, take one or both

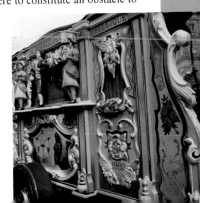

Above: Centraal Station
Right: old-time barrel organ

The Harbour
300 m / 330 yds

•••••• Itinerary 6

Het IJ

NOORD 5

of the ferries that cross the IJ channel from a pier at the rear of Centraal Station. Unusually for Amsterdam, the crossings are free of charge. The **Buiksloterwegveer** is a covered landing craft that crosses the channel in two minutes, while the **Adelaarswegveer** looks more like a real boat, and takes all of three minutes for its crossing to a point further east. Both vessels will transport your bicycle.

River Traffic

On the way across the quite busy channel you will probably intersect the wakes of canal boats and pleasure boats, and perhaps a visiting warship or an ocean-going cruise liner. Watch out for the Royal Dutch Shell office tower on the north bank – its windows sparkle in the sunlight.

There is not a great deal to see in Amsterdam North, which is mostly a modern residential area, and you probably won't want to spend much time on the north bank. Ferries come and go every few minutes, so you should not have very long to wait before returning to Centraal Station.

Take the No, 35 bus from the stop outside Centraal Station on De Ruijterkade (beside the Holland International canal-boat jetty) to Tasmanstraat. Or you might decide to walk there; the road has a good view of the harbour. There are no famous monuments or tourist attractions in this neighbourhood – the point is to experience the old harbour's ambience. On the left side of Tasmanstraat is a cramped area – full of characterful warehouses, docks, small boatyards and other harbour installations – that is being converted into residences.

Take a stroll down Houtmankade, passing the children's playground on

Zoutkeetsplein, until you reach the end of Houtmankade, then turn left onto Schiemanstraat and Sloterdijkstraat. Walk across the narrow bridge over Prinseneilandsgracht, to Galgenstraat (where a wooden clog has been pinned to the window frame at No. 10) and Kleine Bickersstraat. Then, by way of Bickersstraat and Jonkerplein, walk under the railway bridge to the bus stop on Haarlemmer Houttuinen.

Having acquainted yourself with the harbour, take the No. 22 bus back to Centraal Station. You can either get out and walk to Kattenburgerplein, or continue there on the No. 22 (a break at Centraal Station gives you another opportunity to sample the delights served up by the station buffet). Once at Kattenburgerplein, cross to the **Nederlands Scheepvaart Museum** (Maritime Museum, 1 Kattenburgerplein; Tues–Sat 10am–5pm, and Mon Jun–Sept, Sun noon–5pm; entrance fee). Housed in the former Amsterdam Admiralty building, dating from 1656, the museum documents and celebrates Holland's sea-faring history, with a pronounced emphasis on the 17th century, when the country was one of the world's great sea powers. Here you will find a fascinating selection of paintings, models, marine instruments, and a vast array of other exhibits – including real ships.

A full-scale replica of the 17th-century Dutch East Indiaman, the *Amsterdam*, is moored to a jetty outside the museum. It presents a fantastic sight, a squat yet elegant mountain of timber surmounted by three tall masts and threaded with a tracery of rigging. Breezes from the nearby shipping channel roil the water and set the *Amsterdam* swaying gently at her moorings. Below decks, in the crew's quarters and cargo hold, the vessel's timbers creak

and groan alarmingly, creating an evocative impression of conditions on such a craft when rounding the Cape of Good Hope and facing the full force of a storm in the turbulent waters of the Indian Ocean.

Science and Technology

Follow the waterfront around Kattenburgerplein, past a sculpture of Amphitrite, to the long stairway that leads up to the wonderful **New Metropolis Science and Technology Centre** (2 Oosterdok; July and Aug: daily 10am–9pm; Sept–June: Mon–Thur 10am–6pm, Fri–Sun 10am–9pm; entrance fee),. Like its many interactive exhibits, the centre's futuristic architecture reflects the high-tech experience of life in the 21st century. All exhibits at this child-friendly place have explanation in English and there are guided tours.

Top: mooring a boat at the harbour
Right: at the Maritime Museum

7. THE CANALS BY CANAL BIKE *(see pull-out map)*

Take a mini-cruise, riding a water-bike along the canals.

Start at the canal-bike mooring on Prinsengracht, next to Anne Frank Huis. You can start at any of Canal Bike's four moorings (the other three are at Leidseplein, Keizersgracht/Leidsestraat and the Rijksmuseum) and return the bike to any of them. Allow for two or three hours.

Amsterdammers look down their noses at water bikes; tourists seem to love them. Amsterdam is best seen from the water, and as captain of a two- or four-person water bike you can navigate your way through the canal network. For information, contact **Canal Bike** (24 Weteringschans, tel: 626 5574).

You will be told the rules when you hire a bike: you cannot ride on the IJ channel or the River Amstel, and there may be other places that are out of bounds. You can buy a brochure and map that outline five good routes. The

canals can get busy, so watch out for potential problems, particularly when passing under bridges. In bad weather, the bikes, which are safe and unsinkable, can be fitted with rainshields.

Side-canals

Pedal southwards along Prinsengracht, past Lauriergracht, Looiersgracht and then Passeerdersgracht. Take the opportunity to turn into one or more of these bways – the quiet side-canals can be compelling. At Leidsegracht, you can turn off, but it's better to plough straight ahead, under Leidsestraat, until you reach the pretty **Spiegelgracht**, where you should turn right. Continue to the end then turn left under the bridge into Lijnbaansgracht.

Turn right after the **Mankind** cafe at the first corner on the right to a short, dark and dank canal alongside Weteringstraat. Keep going under the Weteringspoort Bridge and re-emerge with the Rijksmuseum ahead. Turn right into Singelgracht, at whose mooring you can leave your bike. If you continue the ride you'll find a greener canalside, with overhanging trees in the gardens of villas that are now mostly offices.

You're entering busier waters now, as you pass the lido and its water-front cafe terrace, then Leidseplein and the *jugendstil* **American Hotel**, opposite which is another canal-bike mooring where you can deposit the bike.

Otherwise, to complete the circuit, pass the **Bellevue Theater** and the **De la Mar Theater** and turn right into Leidsegracht, which brings you back to Prinsengracht and a straight run back to Westermarkt.

Above: local people don't like them, but water-bikes are popular with visitors
Above Right: trams are fast and fun

8. AMSTERDAM BY TRAM *(see pull-out map)*

Riding Amsterdam's trams is fun, fast and convenient. This express-tram itinerary passes many of the city's highlights, and the new business and residential districts on the outskirts. It takes about two hours.

Start from Centraal Station. Take the blue tram No. 5 from the stop to your left as you face the station. Buy a 'strippenkaart' (strip ticket) from the on-board ticket machine or use one you bought previously. This itinerary covers three zones, so insert the fourth available strip in one of the on-board validation machines.

As the tram emerges from Centraal Station, keep an eye open for the 1629 brown cafe **De Karpershoek** to your right on the corner of Martelaars-gracht. The tram rolls along Nieuwezijds Voorburgwal and stops at a build-ing with pear-shaped towers that was formerly the main Post Office and is now the **Magna Plaza** shopping centre. To your left is the rear of the **Royal Palace.** Further ahead, towards Spui, the tram passes the **Amsterdams Historisch Museum** on your left.

Note the excellent Indonesian restaurant **Kantjil en de Tijger** beside the tram stop at Spui. You swing around Koningsplein and into **Leidsestraat**, which is a notable shopping street. The tram stops on the bridges across **Keizersgracht** and **Prinsengracht**, giving passengers a fine view along the canals. Leidseplein is one of the places at which you might alight, for a stroll around Amsterdam's most happening square. The **Stadsschouwburg** (City Theatre) is the red-brick building beside the stop, and the *jugendstil* **American Hotel** the multi-turreted extravaganza that follows it.

As the tram turns hard left onto Stadhouderskade, get ready for some rapid-fire switches of attention from right to left and back again. To your left is the **Holland Casino Amsterdam**, then to your right the entrance to **Vondelpark**. You veer into Hobbemastraat, with the illustrious **Pieter Cornelisz Hooftstraat** shopping thoroughfare and **Coster Diamonds** to your right, and the **Rijksmuseum** to your left, then into Paulus Potterstraat, where, in quick succession out of the left-side window, you will notice the

Above: it's better by tram

Van Gogh Museum and the **Stedelijk Museum** of modern-art. Now the tram turns left into Van Baerlestraat, where the **Concertgebouw** lies to your right and the long vista of Museumplein to your left.

Into the Suburbs

Further along, you turn right on a road leading to Beethovenstraat, from which point there are fewer landmarks to see and you can relax. Now the tram, liberated from the city centre's constricted streets, picks up the pace. The view is one of apartment blocks, at least until you reach the big, blue-glass-fronted **World Trade Centre Amsterdam**, known locally as the Blauwe Engel (Blue Angel). Other modern office towers line the adjacent motorway until the tram turns left into Buitenveldertselaan, with the **Vrije Universiteit** (Free University) to your right – look out for the giant bicycle parking lot in front of the university.

   The tram rushes ever faster through the dormitory suburbs of Buitenveldert and Amstelveen, until it takes a hard right off Beneluxbaan and stops a few seconds later at the terminus beside the **Amstelveen Shopping Centre**. This is a good place for out-of-town shopping although, predictably, it lacks the character of the city centre. If you're feeling peckish, walk just a few metres to the **Vroom & Dreesmann** department store. V&D has a justifiably popular sandwich counter, at which you can order your choice of fillings before watching the sandwich being prepared on fresh-baked bread in front of you.

Return Journey

You might, for the sake of variety, decide to return on a different tram, in which case walk to the stop on Beneluxbaan. The imposing white building you pass on the way is another modern art centre – the **Cobra Museum** (1–3 Sandebergplein; Tues–Sun 11am–5pm), dedicated to the art movement after which it is named. Take the rapid tram No. 51 in the direction of the Centraal Station. You retrace the previous route as far as the World Trade Centre before passing the enormous **RAI Congressgebouw** (Congress Centre) to your left and, by way of any number of tortuous twists and turns and subterranean tunnels, join the metro line inbound to the city centre. Beyond **Amstel Station**, the line runs underground, taking you quickly back to Centraal Station.

9. BY BICYCLE ALONG
THE RIVER AMSTEL *(see pull-out map)*

If you have so far resisted the temptation to join Amsterdam's legions of cyclists for fear of the swirling traffic, get on your bike for this itinerary. Cycle along a fairly quiet riverside route and emerge in the countryside on the way to the pretty village of Ouderkerk aan de Amstel. Allow four or five hours, depending on how fast you cycle. There are no sites to visit, but you will probably want to stop at a cafe or restaurant.

Start at Waterlooplein, which is served by tram lines 9, 14 and 20 and, stopping at the metro station, the metro and sneltram lines 51, 53 and 54.

The best place from which to rent a bicycle in this district is **Mac Bike** (2 Mr Visserplein, tel: 020-620 0985), off the north side of Waterlooplein. *(For details on Waterlooplein see Itinerary 11, The Jewish Quarter, page 48.)* Once you have chosen a suitable model, cycle to the right (east) bank of the **River Amstel**, passing but not crossing the **Blauwbrug** (Blue Bridge) connecting Waterlooplein and Amstelstraat. Houseboats are moored along the river here and the scene on the water is likely to be quite busy. Continue to the **Magere Brug**, the 'Skinny Bridge' over the Amstel, an 18th-century replacement for the original 17th-century bridge. Note the fine local eatery **De Magere Brug** (81 Amstel), whose guest book was signed by the Scottish pop singer Rod Stewart, with the commendation, 'Nice ham 'n' eggs'.

Cross to the left bank and continue south. You should be able to see the **Theater Carré**, where Stewart had been performing, on the other side of

the water. Continue over the tram lines on Sarphatistraat. You need to describe a convoluted route now, diverting around a break in the riverside road, over busy Stadhouderskade and back to the river at **Amsteldijk**.

Keep pedalling south, enjoying the ambience, until you reach the **Berlage Brug**, where the traffic becomes busier. At **Martin Luther King Park** most of the traffic swings away on President Kennedylaan, leaving you still on the Amsteldijk, which is now almost rural, with houseboats in place of cottages.

The thundering noise you begin to hear up ahead might sound like a Niagara-sized waterfall, but is actually the traffic on the A10 Ringweg Zuid bridge.

You're in the countryside now, passing Amstel Park and a pretty, if kitsch, scene of a windmill complete with a statue of Rembrandt. Beyond this is a great little cafe, **Het Kalfje**, whose riverside terrace is unfortunately on the other side of the road. (There used to be a road sign that read, 'Caution: Waiter Crossing'.)

The river is scenic and tranquil as you pass villas and cottages en route to **Ouderkerk aan de Amstel**. This village has plenty of restaurants and cafes with waterside terraces, most of them owned by Holland's first family of cuisine, the Fagels. The village is good for exploring by bike. If you want to eat here, you can do no better than the **Paardenburg** (5 Strandvlietlaan).

Left: technology comes alive over the Amstel
Right: three on a bike

Return Ride

Switch to the right bank to return. This road – Ouderkerkerdijk – passes through some delightful hamlets; look out for another windmill. Recross the river at the **Utrechtse Brug**, which marks your return to the urban scene. Take Amsteldijk to the Berlage Brug. At this point you can either recross and cycle to **Amstel Station**, from where you and your bike can board a metro to Waterlooplein, or cycle back along whichever bank takes your fancy.

10. THE JORDAAN *(see map, p47)*

This working-class district has been subject to gentrification, but plenty of its original charm remains. Allow two hours for this afternoon stroll.

Start this itinerary beside the Noorderkerk at Noordermarkt. This is not on any of the city's tram or bus routes; to get there from Centraal Station, walk along Prins Hendrikkade to Haarlemmer Houttuinen and Prinsengracht.

The great golden-age canals of 17th-century Amsterdam were intended to serve the homes of the landed nobility and wealthy merchants; the artisans and labourers were consigned to the **Jordaan** – a grid of streets and narrow canals cut east–west along the course of existing polders (drainage ditches). The Jordaan's name may derive from the French *jardin* (garden), possibly in reference to the market gardens maintained by the original inhabitants. For a description of the Noordermarkt and Noorderkerk (North Church), see *Itinerary 1: The Golden Age Canals, page 23*.

Walk to **Brouwersgracht** (the Brewers' Canal), with its houseboats and rows of old warehouses, now converted into chic apartments. If you want a coffee or beer, try the traditional brown cafe **'t Papeneiland** (2 Prinsengracht) on the corner. Otherwise turn left on Brouwersgracht, past a sculpture of the writer Theo Thijssen (1879–1943). Across the water the modern Blauwe Burgt apartment block exemplifies the way new and old are conjoined along the canals.

Go as far as Palmgracht, onto which you should turn left. Notice the sculpted turnip on the gable at No. 28, a house dating from 1648. Then turn left into Palm Dwarsstraat and continue walking along Tweede Goudsbloemdwarsstraat as far as Lindengracht, which was once a canal. On Saturday, a street market spreads its stalls along this road.

True Amsterdammers

Off Lindengracht you will find **Karthuizerplantsoen**, a square that honours a now-vanished Carthusian monastery. Adjacent Karthuizersstraat has a row of neck-gabled houses (Nos 11, 13, 15, 17 and 19), named after the four seasons: De Lente, De Zomer, De Herfst, and De Winter. The **Huys-Zitten-Weduwe-Hofje** at Nos 61–191 has a tree-shaded courtyard with a

Above: walking the dogs in one of the many open spaces in and around the city double garden. The small houses here, now largely students' quarters, were once the homes of poor widows. Turn into Tichelstraat, from which you can see the Westerkerk tower in the distance: in much the same way that true London Cockneys must be born within the sound of Bow bells, so Jordaanese must be born within earshot of the Westerkerk bells. Cross Westerstraat, which was also formerly a canal.

Café Stop

Tweede Anjeliersdwarsstraat, on which you should now find yourself, has an excellent, brown-cafe-style restaurant, **De Eettuin**, at No. 10. (There are lots of cafes and small designer shops in this neighbourhood.) Drop down a block to Eerste Tuindwarsstraat and Eerste Egelantiersdwarsstraat. On the way, between Tuinstraat and Egelantiersstraat, a passage on the right leads to the **Claes Claesz Hofje**: two attractive little courtyards surrounded by tiny flats.

Turn right on Egelantiersgracht, a quiet canal lined with some fascinating 17th- and 18th-century houses. On this corner, the hardware store at Nos 2–6 is an example of Amsterdam-School architecture dating from 1927. Beside it is another excellent old brown café, **'t Smalle**, with a canal side terrace. There are three beautiful bell gables at Nos 61–65, one of which features a carved falcon. Don't miss the **Andrieshofje** at Nos 107–45, where a corridor lined with blue-and-white tiles leads into a flower-bedecked courtyard.

Retrace your steps, right into Tweede Leliedwarsstraat, and continue to Bloemgracht – one of the most impressive of Jordaan's canals. From here you can see the Westerkerk tower off to your left above the rooftops. The carved gablestones at No 81 and 77, dating back to 1642, represent a townsman, a countryman and a seaman.

To end your afternoon, walk back towards **Prinsengracht,** turn right, and cross the bridge over the canal to the **Rum Runners** Caribbean cafe-restaurant (277 Prinsengracht), for cocktails, followed by dinner.

Above: at 't Papeneiland brown café

11. THE JEWISH QUARTER
(see map right)

The once-thriving community of the Jodenbuurt (Jewish Quarter) was mostly wiped out in the Holocaust, but a number of Jewish elements remain in this distinctive part of the city. Allow for a four-hour walk.

Start at Waterlooplein, served by tram lines 9, 14 and 20, and by metro.

This itinerary begins with the multifarious offerings of the **flea market** (Mon–Sat 10am–4pm) on the west and north sides of **Waterlooplein**. In the 19th century the Dutch author Multatuli wrote of the market: 'There were headless nails, toothless saws, bladeless chisels, locks without springs, keys without locks, hooks without eyes and eyes without hooks, buckles without prongs…' You may well find that nothing much has changed, except that there are many genuine bargains among

the mess. Whether you're looking to buy or merely taking in the ambience, the market is great fun.

'Stop the Stopera'

Just as construction of the metro line under your feet was the cause of rioting in the 1970s, so in the 1980s the nascent 'Stopera' building brought protesters and water cannon back onto the streets. The name was derived from the **Stadhuis** (Town Hall) and the new **Opera** (better known as the **Muziektheater**) that were built on the square. 'Stop the Stopera' was the popular, but ultimately ineffectual, slogan; both institutions are now firmly established, and the Muziektheater is a star in the city's cultural firmament.

Cross the square and walk through the short Turfsteeg alley to the **Joods Historisch Museum** (Jewish Historical Museum, 2–4 Jonas Daniël Meyerplein; daily 11am–5pm; entrance fee) in the former Ashkenazi Synagogue. This house of worship was restored following its destruction in World War II. The museum has artefacts pertaining to the 400-year history and culture of Holland's Jews. The displays feature paintings, books, and religious and household objects.

Cross Mr Visserplein to the lovely **Portuguese Synagogue** (3 Mr Visserplein; Apr–Oct: Sun–Fri 10am–12.30pm, 1–4pm; Nov–Mar: Mon–Thur 10am–12.30pm, 1–4pm, Sat 10am–3pm, Sun 10am–noon), dating from 1665. It was built by Sephardi Jews fleeing the latest bout of reli-

Above: flea-market mannequin
Right: spring blooms in Amsterdam

gious persecution in Spain and Portugal. Outside the synagogue, the Dock-worker Monument honours Amsterdam workers – not just dockers – who went on strike in February 1941 to protest against the Nazis' deportation of the city's Jews. The occupiers' retribution was characteristically brutal.

Take Weesperstraat across the bridge over the Nieuwe Herengracht to the garden, on the right side of the road. Here another statue relating to the Holocaust, a 1950 monument in the form of an altar, is dedicated to the Dutch people who protected and hid Jews during the war. Retrace your steps and recross Mr Visserplein, past the neoclassical **Moses en Aaronkerk** on the corner of Waterlooplein. This Roman Catholic church was built on a spot where, in the 16th century, Catholics worshipped in secret to avoid the Calvinist authorities. At 17 Waterlooplein, the **Holland Experience** (daily 10am–8pm; entrance fee) presents a multimedia film show to demonstrate some of the country's most pertinent features. These include a simulation of what would happen if the sea dykes collapsed, complete with flowing water.

Continue to Jodenbreestraat and Sint-Antoniesbreestraat, which was once the centre of Jewish life in the city and is now partly redeveloped. You might want to visit the **Museum het Rembrandthuis** (Rembrandt House Museum, 4–6 Jodenbreestraat; Mon–Sat 10am–5pm, Sun 1–5pm), where the artist lived and worked until his bankruptcy in 1658.

Return to Waterlooplein and pass the Stadhuis to the black-marble **Jewish Resistance Fighters' Memorial** on the corner of the square. Finish at the stylish **Grand Café Dantzig** next to the memorial.

12. AMSTERDAMSE BOS   *(see pullout map)*

For a breath of fresh air outside the confines of the city, visit Amsterdamse Bos, the wooded park on the southern outskirts. This is the countryside on the city's doorstep. Take a picnic. Allow at least four hours.

From Centraal Station take the No. 16 tram to the terminus at Stadionplein.

If your stay in Amsterdam is long enough to accommodate an out-of-town excursion, **Amsterdamse Bos** (Amsterdam Wood) makes for a nice day out. Facing you as you descend from the tram at Stadionplein is the **Olympisch Stadion**, Amsterdam's old Olympic Stadium, which had its 15 minutes of fame during the 1928 Olympics. It is unlikely to be open, but you can see how Olympic Games showcases have changed in 70 years.

In the summer you can reach the *bos* by old-style tram from Haarlemmer-meerstation just north of the stadium. This service is courtesy of the Electric Tramline Museum, whose amazing collection of antique trams has been drawn from various European countries.

Otherwise, from the bus stop on Stadionplein, take any bus going out of town for several stops along Amstelveenseweg to the entrance to Amsterdamse Bos. Or you could walk there under the viaduct of the A10 Ring Road and past the **Vrij Universiteit Hospital**, but you might want to save your time and shoe leather for the park.

Although it might seem entirely natural, Amsterdamse Bos, like so much of the Netherlands, is artificial. In 1928 the Amsterdam municipality elected to transform a series of polders to the south of the city into a public park, not least to provide employment – this was the era of the Great Depression.

All the work was completed by men and horses, with nothing left to machinery.

Today the 800-ha (2,000-acre) *bos* is an important ecological site. It serves as the home to numerous species of birds, insects and small animals. For instance, it supports no fewer than 700 different species of beetle. Moreover, the *bos* incorporates almost 160km (100 miles) of footpaths, and some 48km (30 miles) of bicycle paths.

Café Bosrand beside the entrance is a reasonable place for lunch. Take Koenenkade into the park, crossing the line of the Elektrische Museum Tramlijn (on Sunday in the summer an old tram wends its way on this line from Haarlemmermeer Station near Stadionplein). At the Bosbaan take a right over the canal bridge, then onto another bridge over a shallow inlet to the edge of **Nieuwe Meer**, a surprisingly tranquil lake given that it is situated on the edge of the busy ring road and Schiphol Airport.

Messing about in Boats

Follow the path to the **Roeibaan**, a 2-km (almost 1 mile) rowing course. At the eastern end of this long, straight stretch of water is a cluster of rowing stations and pavilions, where on most days you will see rowing enthusiasts setting up their craft. Here there is another café, **Bosbaan**, which has a terrace that overlooks the course. Follow the Roeibaan to its western end (which is the start of the rowing course). En route you will probably pass a long line of anglers. Turn right at the end and follow the signs for the **Bosmuseum** (56 Koenenkade; daily 10am–5pm; tel: 643 1414; admission free). Here you can trace the park's history and learn about the diverse wildlife that can be found here. Next to the museum is a self-service restaurant, **Boerderij Meerzicht**, which is probably the best of the park's eateries, especially for light fare such as pancakes.

Above: picnic in the Amsterdamse Bos

Retrace your steps past the western end of the rowing course and take the tree-lined path to the big **Grote Vijver** pond and the nearby, 1,500-seat **Open-luchttheater** (Open-air Theatre), where there are often performances on summer evenings. You can hire boats and paddle around the pond or simply enjoy the scenery and fresh air. Don't forget you have to walk the length of the Roeibaan again to reach the exit and catch the bus back to the centre.

13. LEIDSEPLEIN *(see pullout map)*

The Leidseplein area constitutes the beating heart of the city's nightlife, with many of its most popular bars, restaurants and nightclubs all in close proximity. The area never really closes, so if you have the energy you can dance the night away and still be up to greet the dawn and have breakfast. This tour highlights the most interesting possibilities.

Start at Leidseplein, reached by trams 1, 2 and 5 from Centraal Station.

When planning a night out on **Leidseplein**, it can be difficult knowing where to start. The square is a central landmark and a clockwise circuit will help to familiarise you with its attractions. One of the foremost of these, at No. 15, is the **Bulldog Palace**. Far from being a regal palace, this gruff and bristly standard-bearer of the genre is one of the 'smoking coffee shops' for which Amsterdam is famous. 'Smoking' refers to marijuana and hashish, both of which have been legal in the Netherlands for a number of years. Numerous foreign pot smokers make their way to Amsterdam specifically to puff their way through as much of these soft drugs as they can.

From Cinemas to the Casino

The movies form another major attraction in this neighbourhood. An extension of Leidseplein is a smaller square, **Kleine Gartmanplantsoen** in which,

at Nos 13–25, you will find the seven-screen **City** complex and, just across the road, the four-screen Alfa complex (4 Hirschpassage). Both of these cinemas tend to show Hollywood's latest releases with Dutch subtitles.

Next to the Alfa is one of the best cafe-restaurants in the square – **De Balie** (10 Kleine Gartmanplantsoen), a chic place that serves great snacks on the ground floor and has a good restaurant upstairs. Left of the Balie as you face it is a passage leading to **Max Euweplein**, the home of **Holland Casino Amsterdam**, the city's only legally recognised casino (to gain entry you must be properly dressed and show your passport). Alternatively, the **Comedy Club** (No. 29) is a bar that often features fast-paced humour in English.

Right: hanging out in the Bulldog

If seeing and being seen is more your thing, return to Leidseplein. Across Leidsestraat is the *jugendstil* **American Hotel**, whose stylish **Café Américain** is a showcase for Amsterdam's beautiful people. For people-watching on the square, the hotel's street-level **Night Watch** bar is a good bet even though it is a bit removed from the action. A short way along Marnixstraat from here is the four-screen Bellevue-Calypso cinema complex (Nos 400–2).

Across Marnixstraat, back at Leidseplein, the **Stadsschouwburg** (City Theatre) at No. 26 stages most of its dramatic productions in Dutch, but it does sometimes feature visiting musicals from London's West End and New York's Broadway, as well as sundry dance performances. Also located in Leidseplein, at No. 12, is the excellent **Boom Chicago Theater**, which specialises in improvisational comedy, much of it in English, that can be enjoyed over dinner.

Blast from the Past

For a less formal, more alternative experience, take Lijnbaansgracht next to the theatre to **Melkweg** (Milky Way, No. 234). The heyday of this entertainment mecca was 30 years ago, at the height of the hippie era, when various big-name psychedelic American and British rock bands would ply their lengthy, acid-fuelled musical extravaganzas here. These days the Milky Way is constantly reinventing its multimedia persona – it has a restaurant, coffee shop, bar, art centre, dance theatre, disco, cinema and concert hall among its facilities.

Adjacent to the Stadsschouwburg and the Boom Chicago is a mass of busy cafés, the terraces of which extend into the square in sunny weather (and sometimes when it is raining too). Though they are all very much alike, the brown-cafe-style **Reijnders** at No 6 is particularly recommended.

A short distance further along the street, at No. 10, **De Oesterbar** is a very popular seafood restaurant, while **Akbar** at 15 Korte Leidsedwarsstraat is a fairly reliable Indian option. On the other side of the square, on the continuation of Korte Leidsedwarsstraat, you will find **The Rookies**, at Nos

145–47, is a popular smoking coffee shop comparable to The Bulldog but of an even more mellow disposition.

In a slightly wider zone around Leidseplein, embedded in a blur of cafes, restaurants and neon, are all manner of opportunities to sample live music. Try your luck at the **Bamboo Bar** (115 Lange Leidsedwarsstraat). If you are a jazz aficionado, the music is generally of a high standard at the **Alto Jazz Café** (115 Korte Leidsedwarsstraat). You will find blues aplenty at **Bourbon Street** (6 Leidsekruisstraat); and new styles of music at **Paradiso** (6–8 Weteringschans). If you're willing to take a tram for a couple of stops along Lijnbaansgracht, one of the city's best blues venues, **Maloe Melo**, is within range at No. 63 Lijnbaansgracht.

Left: to your health

14. REMBRANDTPLEIN *(see pullout map)*

Rembrandtplein has a more downmarket reputation than Leidseplein, yet it often seems even more intent on having fun.

Start at Muntplein on the corner of Reguliersbreestraat, which can be reached by Nos 4, 9, 14, 20, 24 and 25 trams.

Take particular care when crossing busy Muntplein to Reguliersbreestraat not to get hit by a tram – especially if you are accustomed to traffic being driven on the left. There are a couple of peep-show joints on this street, but in a field not renowned for its sophistication these venues are on the tacky side. More interesting is the six-screen **Tuschinski Theater Cinema** (26–28 Reguliersbreestraat), housed in an Art Deco masterpiece.

For a Malibu-style bar-restaurant-dance venue, go left on Halve Maansteeg to the Amstel and the **Bayside Beach Club** (Nos 4–6). Here the attempts to evoke the atmosphere promised in its name extends to the uniform of the waitresses – skimpy Stars-and-Stripes bikinis. If Dutch cabaret-theatre appeals, the **Kleine Komedie** (58 Amstel) is a great venue for what is a lively and inventive satirical scene in Holland. A few doors further along on Amstel is **Mulligan's Irish Music Bar** (No. 100) where the music and the *craic* are so authentic you could be downing a pint of Guinness in Dublin.

If the Gaelic experience doesn't appeal, three local options might. The young at heart should keep going to No. 178, where they will find the **Willems Club** dance-bar. Around the corner from here, at Wagenstraat 3, is **Sinners in Heaven**, a trendy dance-club. At the other end of the spectrum is the **Muziektheater**, the city's premier venue for ballet and opera, at 22 Waterlooplein (make your way to the end of Amstel and glance across the river). Those who appreciate the opportunity to walk, or rather dance, on the wild side should turn back along Amstelstraat to No. 24 and **IT**. Though an ostentatiously gay dance-club, it also stages mixed nights.

For something more mainstream, you might want to try **Soul Kitchen** (No. 32) featuring soul classics and pop favourites from the 1960s and 1970s.

Above: Rembrandtplein has any number of restaurants and cafés with terraces

Music Spectrum

Soul Kitchen is not far from **Rembrandtplein**, a brash and brassy square that really comes into its own at night when it is awash with neon. At No. 46 there's a British-style pub, the Old Bell which, although somewhat dreary, at least allows for a restful break. **Café Schiller** (No. 36) is an island of chic. Live music to drink to, and dance to if you can find space, is offered by **Shorts of London**, but you won't win points for being hip. At the seriously smart **Royal Café de Kroon** opposite (No. 17) drinking and dining is accompanied by cool piano music; at **Zilver** (No. 19) it's jazz. For some local flavour there are other cafes in the square where locals and out-of-town Dutch like to assemble for a knees-up to schmaltzy songs.

Turn into Thorbeckeplein where, tucked in among numerous topless bars and 'exotic' floorshows, is a hot-wired jazz venue, the **Heeren van Aemstel** (No. 5). For Caribbean dancing and salsa parties at **Club Margaritas** (Nos 100–14), take Reguliersdwarsstraat at the corner of Rembrandtplein and Thorbeckeplein.

If you have enough stamina left and there's still time before dawn, you can merge this nightlife itinerary with the previous, Leidseplein itinerary. Continue across Vijzelstraat to Leidsestraat at the end of Reguliersdwarsstraat to take in music venues such as **Duivel** (No. 87), **Madelief** (No. 74) for salsa, and **Korte Golf** (No. 41) on the way.

15. RED-LIGHT DISTRICT *(see pullout map)*

This is a place many visitors want to see even if they don't want to participate. One of the best times to come is dusk, when the red lights glow with Japanese-lantern charm on the inky surface of the canals. Allow from one hour to all night.

Start at the Dam outside the Grand Hotel Krasnapolsky. There is no problem about women going around in groups of two or more but a single female might be subject to misrepresentation.

'Cover me. I'm going in,' reads a folksy advert for condoms, a much-requested item of apparel in the red-light district. So, hitch your moneybelt a notch tighter and keep your hands where everybody can see them. We're going in.

Lots of visitors do this kind of itinerary out of curiosity or just for fun. You don't need to worry overmuch about crime as long as you stick to the busier streets. You can banter with the girls in the windows (most of them revel in their role as tourist attractions), but it is inadvisable to try and snap pictures of them unless you are dressed for swimming in the canal.

Take Damstraat at the side of the Krasnapolsky to the canal-side on Oudezijds Voorburgwal, turn left, and you're there. This is a fairly easy introductory step, as business behind the red-fringed windows doesn't start to get brisk until you reach the **Oude Kerk** (Old Church, covered in *Itinerary 4, The Old Centre, page 35*). Turn left into Oudekerksplein, and then left again into Sint-Annendwarsstraat. Sexy Land (No 48), in the shadow of the venerable church, is more or less typical of the fare on offer all over, with private cabins and a live show.

For an even closer experience of the often suffocating atmosphere of the district, stroll down the short Trompetersteeg from Sint-Annendwarsstraat back to Oudezijds Voorburgwal. You have literally to squeeze past the women in the doorways of this constricted alleyway, giving them the ideal opportunity for a friendly form of marketing.

Heart of the Area

Continue past the Oude Kerk and go right across the bridge. Turn right onto **Oudezijds Voorburgwal**, which is really the heart of the surprisingly small red-light district. You might want to saunter into some of the street's many bookshops, video libraries or specialised appliances shops crammed around here. If you do you will encounter knowledgeable specialists in diverse areas of human relationships.

The Sex Palace (No 84) shows a less-than-admirable determination to get to the bottom of its subject matter. Casa Rosso (No 108) proudly considers itself the market leader in live shows. To bolster its cultural credentials it translates this description into several languages (in French, for example, the entertainment on offer sounds like a riverside village near Paris: *Baiser sur scène*).

You will no doubt find a good deal to entertain, horrify, depress or bore you, depending on your slant. My favourite address is the **Amusement Centre** (1 Molensteeg). I always leave thoroughly amused. Try it and see.

Left: where there are red lights in the windows, the entertainment is for adults
Above: just one out of a huge number of different options

Excursions

1. HAARLEM AND ZANDVOORT *(see map p58)*

Haarlem can justifiably claim to share many of Amsterdam's advantages – fascinating history, pleasing atmosphere, 17th-century, golden-age architecture, and plenty of canals – while mostly avoiding the hassles that go with the capital's often eccentric lifestyle. Zandvoort is the destination for Amsterdammers taking a vacation at the seaside. Both towns can be reached easily by train. If it's a sunny day, you might pack swimming gear and suntan lotion for Zandvoort beach.

Start from Amsterdam Centraal Station. There is a train to Haarlem every hour. For Zandvoort, you usually have to change trains at Haarlem on both the outward and return journeys, except in the high season when there are direct trains, too. The journey from Amsterdam to Haarlem takes only 15 minutes, and from Haarlem to Zandvoort another 15 minutes.

As soon as you arrive in **Haarlem**, take a good look around **Haarlem Station**. An Art Nouveau extravaganza dating from 1908, it can be considered a destination in its own right. The moderately priced **Station Restaurant**, situated in the former first-class waiting room, features pristine white tablecloths, conscientious service and, most importantly of all, wonderful cuisine. You might decide to stop here for lunch before going on to Zandvoort, or for dinner on the return journey.

When you emerge onto Stationsplein, walk down Kruisweg, which runs alongside the bus station until you reach the Nieuwe Gracht. Cross over the canal and turn left along the waterside. At the Jansbrug, turn right for a short way on Jansstraat, then quickly left on Korte Jansstraat to the narrow canal called the Bakenessergracht, which is lined by pretty gabled houses, where you turn right at the water.

The Oldest Church

The little alley called Kalverensteeg leads into Goudsmids Pleintje (Goldsmiths' Square), where the goldsmiths' guild was once based, and then to the **Waalse Kerk** (Walloon Church). This, Haarlem's oldest church, was erected in the 16th century by persecuted émigrés – Walloon Protestants and French Huguenots. The church is in the centre of Haarlem's old **Begijnhof**, whose tiny rooms, like their counterparts in Amsterdam, once housed religious lay

Left: an al fresco break in a Haarlem café
Right: cycling on the cobblestones is fun

women. Unlike that city's Begijnhof, however, they have now been put to a far less pious use: the Begijnhof constitutes Haarlem's **Rosse Buurt** (red-light district). Here you will find scantily-clad women waiting behind their windows for customers from the streets.

After circling the church, take Groene Buurt back to the Bakenessergracht and turn right. Look for the white, crowned church spire of the **Bakenesserkerk** behind the roofs on your left; maybe you'll hear its bells as you pass. Bakenessergracht ends at the **River Spaarne**, where, if you wait, you're sure to see big canal boats passing under the Gravenstenenbrug. Cross over to the jetty from where the tour boats of **Woltheus Cruises** (tel: 023-535 7723) leave every hour for a cruise around the canals.

The Oldest Museum

Back on the other side of the bridge, you arrive at the distinguished, neo-classical facade of the **Teylers Museum** (16 Spaarne; Tues–Sat 10am–5pm, Sun 1–5pm; entrance fee) which, dating back to 1778, is the oldest museum in the Netherlands. The Teylers exhibits an eclectic array of items but emphasises science, particularly from the 19th century – everything from fossils and minerals to brass-mounted scientific instruments. You will also find paintings, drawings, medals and coins, and the museum's elegant interior would be worth seeing even if there were no exhibits.

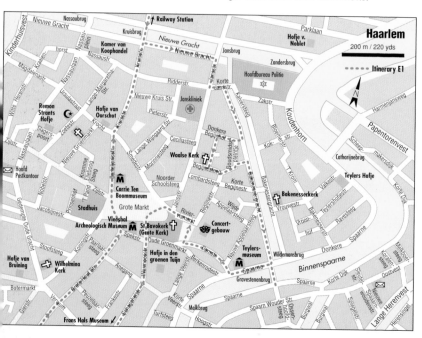

Next door to the Teylers is the **Waag** building (Weigh House), which dates back to 1597. It was built by the Flemish architect Lieven de Key, who designed many of Haarlem's most prominent buildings. It now houses the atmospheric **Herberg De Waag** restaurant (Thur–Tues 5pm–midnight).

Mozart Played Here

Take Damstraat to Oude Groenmarkt, where you will immediately see the imposing bulk of the **Sint-Bavokerk** (Saint Bavo's Church; Mon–Sat 10am–4pm) in front of you. Note the **Concertgebouw** (Concert Hall) on the corner of Klokhuisplein, then turn left into Rivier Vismarkt where, at No. 13, In Den Uiver is an old-style *proeflokaal* (tasting house). Work on the colossal, high-towered Sint-Bavokerk began in the mid-15th century under the direction of the Belgian architect Evert Spoorwater. Handel, Liszt and the 10-year-old Mozart all came to play the church's extraordinary, 1738 **Müller organ**. Inside the church is the tomb of the artist Frans Hals (1580–1666), who lived, worked and died in Haarlem.

Outside is the reasonably-priced seafood restaurant **Haarlem aan Zee** (10 Oude Groenmarkt, tel: 023-531 4848), where you can almost smell the fresh North Sea breeze. Diners sit at booths with brightly-coloured canvas backings, like deckchairs, and choose from oysters, crab, prawns, other *fruits de mer*, and a variety of tasty fish dishes. The square is lined with restaurants and cafes, many of which spread their open-air terraces out onto the street at the first sign of sunny weather.

Take Warmoesstraat at the side of the restaurant, then Schagchelstraat and Groot Heiligland. This is one of the most attractive residential neighbourhoods of Haarlem. The **Frans Hals Museum** (62 Groot Heiligland; Mon–Sat 11am–5pm, Sun 1–5pm; entrance fee), situated among a cluster of old houses originally built for Flemish retired gentlemen, is one of the city's foremost attractions. Hals is noted for paintings such as *The Laughing Cavalier* and *The Gypsy Girl*, but he earned his bread and butter painting portraits of members of the local musketeers' guild. Eight of his pictures hang in the museum, which also exhibits paintings by other Dutch masters, as well as collections of period furniture, fine silverware and ceramics. Look out for the beautiful 18th-century doll's house.

From the museum continue to the canal at the end of Groot Heiligland. Turn right, then second right on Grote Houtstraat, following the street's continuation, Grote Straat – both of which are major shopping streets – to the **Grote Markt**. On your right is the 16th-century **Vleeshal** (meat market),

Above Left: St Bavo's Church spire
Right: in the Frans Hals Museum

which now houses the city's **Archaeological Museum** (Wed–Sun 1–5pm). On the Grote Markt is a sculpture of Laurens Coster, a 15th-century local hero, by the Mechelen artist Louis Royer. Haarlemmers will tell you that it was Coster, not Gutenberg, who invented the printing press. Work on the **Stadhuis** (Town Hall), began in the 14th century; today the building features a tapestry of the Crusades, dating from 1629.

If you want refreshments, **Grand Café Brinkman** at 13 Grote Markt is an ideal place for sitting on a terrace (in good weather) and watching the world go by. Leave the square by Bartel Jorisstraat and continue on Kruisstraat, past the 17th-century **Hofje van Oorschot**, to Kruisweg and back to Haarlem

Station for the trip to the brassy North Sea resort of **Zandvoort**.

The beach

From Zandvoort Station it takes only five minutes to walk to the beach which, in summer, is lined with *paviljoenen* (temporary beach cafe-restaurants). Topless bathing is almost *de rigueur* at Zandvoort – gays and naturists congregate at the south end of the long stretch of excellent sand.

Situated among the dunes just a stone's throw from the coast is **Circuit Park Zandvoort** (63 Burg van Alphenstraat) which, from 1952 to 1985, hosted the Dutch Formula One Grand Prix. Fans hope that what was once a highlight of the national sporting calendar will soon return; in the meantime the circuit still hosts less prestigious car and motorbike racing events.

Aficionados of a quite different type of sport will doubtless appreciate the many charms – roulette, blackjack and so forth – of **Holland Casino Zandvoort** (7 Badhuisplein; daily 1.30pm–2am; entrance fee) behind the central area of the promenade. One of 10 legal casinos in the country, it applies a formal dress code (collar and tie for men) and a minimum age (18). You will be expected to produce your passport if you want to gain entry. Away from the beach but still on the seafront you might choose to tour the **Amsterdamse Waterleidingduinen** – rolling dunes that constitute part of Amsterdam's legendary sea defences. You can roam on paths among the dunes on the sea side, and through woods on the inland side.

Zandvoort is not a particularly good place for shopping, but if you hit the centre of town you will find an array of places to eat, drink and shop. A large number of the shops concentrate on summer clothes, beach accessories and all types of sporting goods that complement the resort's outdoor lifestyle.

Above: in summer Zandvoort's cafes spill onto the pavements

2. THE IJSSELMEER BY BIKE *(see map below)*

A day-long cycling tour to Hoorn following a narrow track between the polders and the IJsselmeer lake, returning to Amsterdam by train.

Start on the ferry that leaves from the rear of Centraal Station. The dykes and polders beside the IJsselmeer get very windy so wear appropriate clothing. This itinerary is a strenuous ride so various exit points are suggested.

It's a good idea to rent your bike on the day before undertaking this itinerary to facilitate an early start. (Try Bike City, Bloemgracht 70, near the Anne Frank Huis.) Cycle to Centraal Station and take the **Adelaarswegveer** (ferry) from the pier by the station, for the short trip to Amsterdam North *(see Itinerary 6: The Harbour, page 39)*. Follow the road directly ahead, Meeuwen-laan, to a roundabout, and turn right onto Nieuwendammerdijk. Opposite a small lake the road veers right onto Schellingwouderdijk, which twists and turns beside the water before becoming Durgerdammerdijk. Follow the dyke road along the tranquil IJsselmeer shore, always keeping the lake on your immediate right. The **IJsselmeer Lake** was once a sea, the Zuiderzee, until the 1930s, when a barrier was constructed to protect the low-lying coastline.

A grandstand view

At **Durgerdam**, the pace of life, which was never that fast, slackens further still. Typical of lakeside villages, Durgerdam huddles below the water level behind the protective dyke, with only its roofs peering over the top. Ride beside the houses or venture up to the dyke-top path, past **Uitdam**, with the sail-studded lake on your right and a grandstand view over the polders on your left.

Above: a classic polder landscape

Turn right at a T-junction onto the causeway leading to **Marken**. (If you're short of time or stamina, turn left instead to skip Marken which, though beautiful, represents a major diversion.) Marken is no longer an island – the causeway connects it to the mainland – but it remains insular. The green-and-white-painted houses of the village are clustered around a tiny harbour to the left of the car park. The remainder of the island is given over to farming. A white lighthouse stands at its tip and *boters* and *skûtsjes* (old-style IJsselmeer sailing ships), ply the waters offshore. For a *koffie en appelgebak met slagroom* (coffee and apple pie with cream) go to **De Taanderij**, a cosy harbour side cafe.

In the summer, you can take an excursion boat, the *Marken Express* (journey time: 25 minutes, frequent service), to Volendam, which means bypassing **Monnickendam** and saving yourself a fair amount of pedalling. Otherwise, retrace your route back across the causeway, and stay on the lake side road as far as Monnickendam. The harbour here has a vast array of pleasure craft, from little dinghies to gleaming, ocean-going luxury cruisers, plus fishing boats.

Volendam and Edam

Stick to the shore and pass through Katwoude on the way to **Volendam**. The populist face of Dutch tourism is on display here. The local people wear traditional costumes – you can have your picture taken wearing clogs and short jackets, or long, flowery aprons and milkmaid hats. Harbour-side fish-stalls do brisk business, especially with smoked IJsselmeer *paling* (eel). If by now you've had enough cycling, this is a good point from which to head back to Amsterdam. But if you still have energy to burn, go inland a short way from the lake dyke to **Edam**, a charming town famed for its *Edammer* cheese. This is another potential exit point – you can keep going west of Edam to nearby **Purmerend**, which has a railway station on the Amsterdam-Hoorn line. If you're game for more, turn right at the canal bridge at **Damplein** in the town centre, and right again to return to the IJsselmeer shore.

Ahead of you is a long, straight run north through the polders beside the lake. The little villages of **Warder**, **Etersheim** and **Scharwoude** are landmarks on the way to **Hoorn**. This, another of the IJsselmeer's emblematic places, is a living reminder of the traders and explorers from Zuiderzee towns in the past – South Africa's Cape Horn takes its name from Hoorn. The town wears its history on its sleeve – witness the care lavished on old sailors' houses, gabled merchants' villas, the Stadhuis (Town Hall) and churches.

It's worth visiting the beautiful inner harbour, the **Binnenhaven**, before taking a restorative drink at the **Hoofdtoren**, a 1532 harbour tower which is now an atmospheric bar, restaurant and grill-bar. Finally, follow the green signs, pointing first to the VVV (local tourism office), then to the station.

Above: traditional dress in Marken
Above Right: an old-fashioned touch in The Hague

excursions

3. THE HAGUE *(see map below)*

A day trip by train to The Hague to see the centres of political power, and to stroll along the seafront at the chic resort of Scheveningen.

From Amsterdam Centraal Station take the Inter City (IC) train to Den Haag Centraal Station (not to be confused with Den Haag HS Station). There are two trains every hour, and the journey takes 48 minutes.

The Hague is Holland's seat of government – Amsterdam is the commercial capital. In contrast with Amsterdam's laid-back, anything-goes approach,

The Hague is elegant and refined. Commonly known as Den Haag (its official name is 's-Gravenhage), it seems less quintessentially Dutch than Amsterdam and, as befits the home of royalty, politicians and bureaucrats, it is well-heeled and a trifle smug.

A Monstrous Mall

Emerging from Centraal Station into the broad Koningin Julianaplein, you can't help but notice, to your right, the monstrous **Babylon** shopping mall and entertainment centre. Pick up a city-centre map from the VVV (local tourism office) on Babylon's ground floor then re-cross Koningin Julianaplein to the traffic lights beside the tram stop. Cross over to Herengracht and Korte Poten. To your left you should be able to see the top of the **De Resident** twin towers complex, part of a gargantuan urban-renewal project under the aegis of several top international architects.

The Hague

500 m / 550 yds

- - - - Itinerary E3

Keep straight on, to **Plein**, an economically named square (*plein* means square), with a statue of William I, Prince of Orange, presiding in the middle. At its northwest corner is Korte Vijverberg, on which, at No. 8, stands the **Mauritshuis Koninklijke Prentenkabinet** (Mauritshuis Royal Picture Gallery; Tues–Sat 10am–5pm, Sun 11am–5pm; entrance fee). In this palace, dating from 1644, is a superb collection of paintings by Rembrandt, Vermeer, Hals, Brueghel, Rubens and other important artists. A 20th-century highlight here is Andy Warhol's portrait of Queen Beatrix.

Houses of Parliament

At the corner of Korte Vijverberg and Plein you will find the entrance to the **Binnenhof** (Inner Court) of the **Houses of Parliament** (Mon–Sat 10am–4pm; last guided tour 3.45pm). Here, in the 13th-century court of the Counts of Holland, is the magnificent, oak-roofed, Gothic **Ridderzaal** (Hall of the Knights), where the sovereign officially opens Parliament every year. Both of the bicameral Parliament's debating chambers, and the Prime Minister's office, are located here. Pass under the western arch to the **Buitenhof**. To your right you will see the ornamental **Hof Vijver** lake, complete with an island and fountain in the middle.

Cross the road and walk to the far end of the Buitenhof. On the left side is the graceful **Passage** shopping arcade. Straight ahead you will see the Dagelijkse Groenmarkt, with the **'t Goude Hooft** cafe-restaurant located in a 16th-century building at No. 13. (The interior was reconstructed in the 20th century following a fire.) If you stop here for lunch, the mussels are excellent, as is the terrace in good weather. A few steps past the restaurant brings you to Kerkplein and the 15th-century Gothic **Grote Kerk** (Great Church).

Leave Kerkplein by Grote Halstraat beside the 1565 Renaissance-style **Oude Stadhuis** (Old Town Hall). Then take the pedestrian-only shopping streets, Oude Molstraat and Papestraat, to Noordeinde, where you turn left. On the road's left side is the neoclassical **Paleis Noordeinde** (Noordeinde Palace). This, the office of Queen Beatrix, is not open to the public. At 98 Noordeinde is **Van Hoogstraten**, an English bookstore and, at No. 121, **It Rains Fishes**, a smart seafood restaurant.

Top: the Houses of Parliament's Inner Court. **Left:** the neoclassical Noordeinde Palace **Right:** there's plenty to do and see in Scheveningen

At the end of Noordeinde, cross over the canal to Zeestraat and the **Panorama Mesdag** (65 Zeestraat; Mon–Sat 10am–5pm, Sun noon–5pm). Painted in 1881, this is a restored, 120-metre (394-ft) circular panoramic painting of Scheveningen, The Hague's seaside resort. You may recall the fascinating panorama when you visit Scheveningen later in the day.

International Court of Justice

Continue to the end of Zeestraat, and cross over to Carnegieplein, on which stands the **Vredespaleis** (Peace Palace; guided tours Mon–Fri 10am, 11am, 2pm, 3pm). Today the palace, built in the first decade of the 20th century with money donated by the Scottish-American philanthropist Andrew Carnegie, houses the International Court of Justice. If by now you have done enough walking, take tram No. 8 from Carnegieplein to Scheveningen.

There is one more place, a model city, that is worth walking to, but it is a fair distance away. Continue on Scheveningseweg, turn right on Arny van der Spuyweg, then left on Dr Aletta Jacobsweg, to arrive right opposite **Madurodam Miniature City** (175 Haringkade; Sept–Mar: 9am–6pm; Mar–Jun 9am–8pm; Jul–Aug 9am–10pm; entrance fee). This enchanting 1:25-scale Dutch city features working lights, bells that ring, planes that taxi on the runway, and trains that run. Children and adults alike love it.

To reach **Scheveningen**, take tram Nos 1 or 9 from Madurodam and get off at Gevers Deynootplein beside the impressive, century-old **Kurhaus Hotel**. Take a walk along the seafront, and out onto the **pier**, where you are surrounded by the North Sea. The **Scheveningen Sea Life Centre** (13 Strandweg; Jul, Aug: daily 10am–8pm; Sept–Jun: daily 10am–6pm) is an aquarium with a glass tunnel surrounded by water, in which you can see sharks and other denizens of the deep in glorious proximity.

A little further along is **Beelden aan Zee** (Sculptures on the Seafront, 1 Harteveltstraat; Tues–Sun 11am–5pm), an open-air modern-sculpture park. In summer you can relax over a coffee or beer at one of the many beach cafes or, alternatively, at the Kurhaus. For dinner, a recommended option is the **Bali** Indonesian restaurant at 1 Badhuisweg, on the street opposite the Kurhaus. Afterwards take tram Nos 1 or 9 back to Centraal Station for the return train journey to Amsterdam.

shopping

Leisure Activities

SHOPPING

Amsterdam is a great city for shopping but not in the same way as New York, London or Paris. Although it has plenty of upscale designer and department stores, the city's intimate, eccentric lifestyle is reflected in its more interesting shopping possibilities. These are to be found in offbeat speciality shops, highly individualistic outlets and in a diverse array of flourishing street markets. If you keep your eyes open in the course of this book's suggested itineraries and excursions, you will doubtless appreciate that the consumer options in Holland, and Amsterdam in particular, are boundless.

Dutch products that make good buys and souvenirs include the following: **flower bulbs** (but be warned that, to import these to some countries, you will be required to show a phytosanitary certificate); Delft and Makkum **pottery** (for high-quality originals, Delft products are labelled 'De Porcelyne Fles', their Makkum equivalents, Tichelaars'); Koninklijke Leerdam **crystal**; **pewter**; **cheese** from specialist shops; **chocolates** from Droste, Van Houten and Verkade; **antiques**; and **diamonds**.

If you are looking for a bargain, the most relevant words are *Solden* (Sales) and *Totale Uitverkoop* (Everything Must Go). Non-EU residents may be able to claim back value-added tax (BTW) paid on purchases. Shops announce their participation in this scheme with a sign in the window. Even if you don't see the sign, it's worth asking, particularly if you buy expensive items.

Thursday evening is *koopavond* (late-shopping), when most shops are open till 9pm. In recent years numerous shops have extended their opening hours to Sunday.

Kalverstraat

Kalverstraat is Amsterdam's most popular shopping thoroughfare. It is full of cheap and cheerful outlets, supplemented by a sprinkling of higher-priced designer stores. While the actual street begins at the Dam and runs to Muntplein, the shopping zone includes its continuation across the Dam in Nieuwendijk, and the adjacent Rokin. The Dam features several department stores, including the **Bijenkorf** (Amsterdam's best), and **Peek & Cloppenburg**. Along the way is **Maison de la Bonneterie** and, at the far end of Kalverstraat. the **Vroom & Dreesman** mid-range department store and **Hema** (Holland's answer to Woolworths).

Beyond the mass of clothes, sports and shoe shops, this district features a branch of **Waterstone's** bookshop chain, at 152 Kalverstraat, and, on the same subject, the **American Book Center** at No. 185. On Rokin, one of the most interesting shops is the **PGC Hajenius** tobacconist at No. 92. If you like your Havanas from a humidor, or want a traditional clay pipe for a souvenir, this is the place for you.

Pieter Cornelisz Hooftstraat

The best place for designer clothes is Pieter Cornelisz Hoofstraat – better known as the 'PC Hooft' *(see Itinerary 3, page 34)* – and the adjoining Van Baerlestraat. You will find this district in the Museum Quarter, not far from the rear of the Rijksmuseum.

Left: one of many individual boutiques
Right: ceramics are always popular

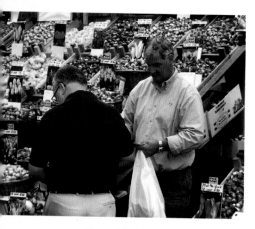

Some of the highly rated outlets on the PC Hooft include: **Azurro**, **Edgar Vos**, **Frans Molenaar**, **Jacques d'Ariege**, **MacGregor**, **Pauw** (and **Pauw Junior** for well-dressed offspring), **Rodier Paris**, **Society Shop**. Here you will also find a branch of the Belgian chocolatier **Godiva**.

Leidsestraat
Leidsestraat runs from Leidseplein, through Koningsplein, and on to Heiligeweg before it joins up with the southern end of Kalverstraat. It is actually an up-market extension of Kalverstraat, with outlets such as Esprit and Cartier. If you're looking for footwear, one of the city's most interesting options is **Shoe-Ba-Loo** at 7 Koningsplein.

Offbeat Shops and Boutiques
There are numerous offbeat stores and designer outlets throughout Amsterdam. The most central and convenient follow the route of the main city-centre canals and the lateral streets that connect the canals, beginning in the Jordaan and continuing to the Spui neighbourhood. From there they jump across Rokin to circumvent the periphery of the red-light district before fading out around Waterlooplein.

Among the most interesting of these shops are: **Animation Art**, 39 Berenstraat; **BLDG Edelsmeden**, 28 Hartenstraat; **Droomdoos**, 1 Oude Leliestraat; **Kitsch Kitchen**, 21 Eerste Bloemdwarsstraat; **Nieuws Innovations**, 297 Prinsengracht; **The Blue Gold Fish**, 17 Rozengracht; and **'t Winkeltje**, 228 Prinsengracht.

Markets
Amsterdam loves street markets. Some are permanent, others appear on a day or two each week. The best markets are: **Albert Cuyp Market**, Albert Cuypstraat (Mon–Sat); **Bio Market**, Noordermarkt, which specialises in organically-grown fruit and vegetables; **Bloemenmarkt**, Singel, the famous floating flower market, where prices are competitive and the flowers excellent (Mon–Sat); **Garden Market**, Amstelveld (Sun); **Textile Market**, Noordermarkt (Mon morning); **Thorbecke Art Market** Thorbeckeplein (Mar–Dec only: Sun) **Waterlooplein Rommelmarkt**, the city's premier flea market, where everything and anything goes (daily; on Sunday in summer the merchandise is very big on antiques and second-hand books).

Spiegelkwartier Antiques
The Spiegelgracht Canal near Leidseplein leads onto Nieuwe Spiegelstraat, which has become an enclave of quality antiques shops.

Diamonds
Amsterdam prides itself on being the 'City of Diamonds'. There is a certain amount of marketing hype about this – Antwerp's diamond trade is worth six times as much. Still, a billion dollars or so of annual sales add up to a sparkling business, and Amsterdam makes it fun to shell out for precious stones. You are unlikely to find much in the way of bargains, though.

Shops associated with the Amsterdam Diamond Foundation are reputable, and they offer tours in which you can see diamond cutting and polishing. The relevant shops are: **Amsterdam Diamond Centre**, 1 Rokin; **Coster**, 2 Paulus Potterstraat; **Gassan**, 173 Nieuwe Uilenburgerstraat; **Stoeltje**, 13 Wagenstraat; and **Van Moppes**, 2 Albert Cuypstraat.

Out of Town
You don't have to trudge around the city centre for shopping. For instance, the Amstelveen mall (see Itinerary 8, Amsterdam by Tram, page 44) is a 40-minute tram ride away from Centraal Station. Branches of **Vroom & Dreesman** and **Hema** are here, along with a range of designer outlets.

Above: the place to buy flower bulbs

EATING OUT

Given that Amsterdam is an adventurous, cosmopolitan city whose population includes a rainbow of ethnic minorities, it is not surprising that its restaurant scene constitutes a smorgasbord of international cuisine. They say you can eat in any language here, which is not far from the truth. The breadth of culinary options is matched by the quality, at all points on the price scale. Moreover, reflecting the Dutch insistence on getting a good return for every euro spent, restaurants tend to represent good value for money.

You should not have any trouble finding a decent place to eat. The old city centre is so thickly populated with restaurants it's a wonder that the residents have anywhere left to live. Although the dense clusters of restaurants around Leidseplein and Rembrandtplein contribute to the colourful atmosphere of both those neighbourhoods, they do not necessarily represent the best of the city's culinary offerings.

Dutch specialities to look out for include Zeeland mussels, raw herring, smoked eel, asparagus, *erwtensoep* (pea-and-ham soup) and *hutspot* (beef-and-vegetable stew), and Indonesian *saté* (grilled meat on skewers, with peanut sauce). Vegetarians in particular should sample the pancakes and *poffertjes* (mini-pancakes).

In general, any restaurant that serves meals cooked according to the Old Dutch style, even if it seems touristy, is a good bet. And, when the weather allows, dining al fresco on a restaurant terrace is recommended. If you are looking for a good, inexpensive meal, try an *eetcafé*, the best of which are traditional brown cafés. By contrast, the grand cafes are sometimes rather pretentious. For something a little more ethnic, try an Indonesian restaurant.

The price categories listed below are based on a three-course meal for two with a bottle or carafe of house wine:

$ = €40–75
$$ = €75–120
$$$ = €120–160.

Most Amsterdam restaurants have a perfectly acceptable *dagschotel* or *dagmenu* (dish or menu of the day), that can cut up to 40 percent off the price of your meal.

Right: specialities of the day

Upscale
Café Américain
American Hotel, 97 Leidsekade
Tel: 020-624 5322
The city's beautiful people like to see and be seen at the landmark that is the Café Américain. The stylish venue – diners are surrounded by Art Deco and *jugendstil* – is complemented by the menu. $$

Excelsior
Hôtel de l'Europe, 2 Nieuwe Doelenstraat
Tel: 020-531 1777
Another restaurant situated in a hotel, the Excelsior offers a smart, fashionable gastronomic experience, in a chandeliered salon with expansive windows overlooking the River Amstel. The menu is Dutch and Continental. $$$

La Rive
Amstel Hotel, 1 Professor Tulpplein
Tel: 020-622 6060
This intimate and elegant river side hotel restaurant specialises in elaborate French cuisine. The service, which is on the formal side, is flawless. Chef Robert Kranenbourg was the first in the Netherlands to earn two Michelin stars. $$$

Traditional
De Blauwe Hollander
28 Leidsekruisstraat
Tel: 020-623 3014
A cheap and cheerful eatery, where diners eat in sociable proximity at large tables in a cosy setting. The dishes – stews, soups, steaks – are straightforward and wholesome, if not particularly exciting. $

Bodega Keyzer
96 Van Baerlestraat
Tel: 020-671 1441
Ideally located for the Concertgebouw, Bodega Keyzer has been serving fine cuisine since 1903, and counts classical musicians and conductors among its regulars. $$

Dorrius
Crowne Plaza Hotel, 5 Nieuwezijds Voorburgwal
Tel: 020-620 0500
Traditional Dutch food in a wood-beamed setting carved out of 19th-century canal houses. Specialities include *hutspot* (stew), duck, deer, and lamb sausage. $$

Haesje Claes
273 Spuistraat
Tel: 020-624 9998
You don't get more homely than this old-fashioned restaurant, which fully merits the prized description *gezellig* (that cosy, welcoming, specifically Dutch quality). The steaks are particularly recommended. $

Pancake Bakery
191 Prinsengracht
Tel: 020-625 1333
This converted 17th-century canal side ware-house does an enormous, typically Dutch, range of outsize savoury and sweet pancakes. Particularly recommended for children. $

D'Vijff Vlieghen
294 Spuistraat
Tel: 020-624 8369
D'Vijff Vlieghen (The Five Flies) wends its way through five old gabled houses, and six dining rooms, each with a different slant on Old Dutch style. $$

Brown-Cafe Style
De Belhamel
60 Brouwersgracht
Tel: 020-622 1095
De Belhamel looks like a brown cafe from the outside but the interior is much more elegant than most such places. Continental cuisine with a classical-music backdrop. $$

De Magere Brug
81 Amstel
Tel: 020-622 6502
De Magere Brug is an old-fashioned neighbourhood restaurant that often caters to performers at the local Theater Carré. $

De Prins
124 Prinsengracht
Tel: 020-624 9382
There's no friendlier place in Amsterdam than De Prins, which might explain why, at peak times, you will probably have to wait for a free table. Moreover, the cuisine, which is both good and stylish, represents very good value for money. $

Above: traditional Dutch fare

Fashionable restaurants

Grand Café Luxembourg
24 Spuistraat
Tel: 020-620 6264
The Grand Café Luxembourg is, as its name suggests, possibly too smart for its own good. Nevertheless, it has earned its place as one of the smartest restaurants on the Amsterdam scene. Its menu includes a number of dishes taken from some of the city's favourite eateries. $$

Moko
12 Amstelveld
Tel: 020-626 1199
If it's a warm summer evening, Moko (formerly Kort) features one of the best terraces in Amsterdam. The fusion food complements the location – the seafood is particularly good. $$

Pier 10
De Ruyterkade, Pier 10
Tel: 020-624 8276
Located on a pier just to the rear of Centraal Station, this harbourside restaurant is both small and popular enough to make advance reservations essential. The menu, which changes with the seasons, places a strong emphasis on fish. $$

Royal Café De Kroon
17 Rembrandtplein
Tel: 020-625 2011
The Royal Café De Kroon is arguably the finest of the grand cafes, not least due to an excellent position overlooking Rembrandtplein. Both the cuisine and the decor are an amalgamation of Continental and Caribbean, and a youthful palm-court orchestra plays at weekends. $$

Vertigo
Film Museum, 3 Vondelpark
Tel: 020-612 3021
Vertigo might seem like an incongruous name for a restaurant set in a basement but the reference – one of many that might appeal to film fans – is to the Alfred Hitchcock movie rather than any fear of heights. The food is Mediterranean-inspired and in good weather you can eat outdoors on one of the finest terraces in town. $$

Wildschut
1–3 Roelof Hartplein
Tel: 020-676 8220
This permanently trendy cafe-restaurant has a pavement terrace that is good for catching some late-afternoon sunshine, which might explain its popularity with after-hours office workers. The food ranges from bar snacks to well-prepared international dishes. $–$$

Ethnic

Edo Japanese Steakhouse
Grand Hotel Krasnapolsky,
9 Dam Square
Tel: 020-554 6096
A superb, showy *teppanyaki* experience. $$

Falafel Koning
2 Reguliersssteeg
Tel: 020-421 1423
It's worth taking the trouble to find this little gem of a place in a narrow alley facing the Tuschinski Theater Cinema. The falafel speciality is the best in the city, the decor is minimalist to the point of non-existent. $

Kantjil en de Tijger
291 Spuistraat
Tel: 020-620 0994
The menu and atmosphere are both cool and refined. The cuisine constitutes a kind of Indonesian nouvelle cuisine. $$

Morita-Ya
18 Zeedijk
Tel: 020-638 0756
Despite its cramped interior, this Japanese restaurant on the edge of the red-light district is excellent. The sushi is superb and, when they are not too busy, the staff might offer you tips on how to prepare it. Or cook your own razor-thin beef at your table. $$

Right: coffee shops abound

Rose's Cantina
38 Reguliersdwarsstraat
Tel: 020-625 9797
Rose's Cantina is a Tex-Mex temple of fun
that is virtually always busy, bustling and
convivial. The food is hardly top-notch, and
your meal may take a long time to arrive,
but you can pass the time with a jug or two
of margaritas. $

Sama Sebo
27 Pieter Cornelisz Hooftstraat
Tel: 020-662 8146
Sama Sebo serves classic Indonesian fare,
the authenticity of which is complemented
by a profusion of mats made from rushes
and batik. Take your pick from the *rijsttafel*
(rice table) – a selection of 20 or 30 little
dishes that represent a cross-section of
Indonesian cuisine. $$

Speciaal
142 Nieuwe Leliestraat
Tel: 020-624 9706
This popular Indonesian restaurant in the
Jordaan lives up to its name. The decor
assumes a traditional tropical style and the
food is authentic. Speciaal is one of the best
places in town to try *rijsttafel*. $

Traiterie Grekas
311 Singel
Tel: 020-620 3590
The culinary offerings compensate for the
lack of space. There are only four tables, so
you may have to settle for a takeaway. $

Vegetarian
Bolhoed
64 Prinsengracht
Tel: 020-626 1803
Bolhoed serves international dishes with a
meat-free slant. The staff take an admirably
breezy approach. $

Golden Temple
126 Utrechtsestraat
Tel: 020-626 8560
Some patrons come to the Golden Temple
for the excellent salad buffet, others for the
main courses – featuring creative Indian,
Middle Eastern and Mexican cuisine. $

Haarlem
Ma Brown's
31–33 Nieuwe Groenmarkt
Tel: 023-531 5829
Given the traditional British nature of Ma
Brown's cuisine, the food is surprisingly
sophisticated. Afternoon teas are served on
the first and third Sunday of the month. $$$

De Pêcherie Haarlem aan Zee
10 Oude Groenmarkt
Tel: 023-531 4848
An excellent choice for lovers of seafood,
situated just off the Grote Markt. The marine
decor is redolent of a good-weather day on
the beach at nearby Zandvoort. $$

The Hague
Bali
1 Badhuisweg, Scheveningen
Tel: 070-346 9713
A strong contender for the country's finest
Indonesian restaurant, which, in the
Netherlands, is quite an accolade. Bali is
situated in The Hague's North Sea resort of
Scheveningen. It enjoys a traditional set-
ting and does a superb *rijsttafel*. $$

't Goude Hooft
13 Groenmarkt
Tel: 070-350 2434
A somewhat old-fashioned, rustic restaurant situated in the heart of The Hague, 't
Goude Hooft underwent a modern reconstruction following a fire. Its extensive menu
covers everything from bar snacks to full-
scale traditional Dutch meals. $–$$

Above: a toast to some of the best beer in the world
Right: a romantic night setting

NIGHTLIFE

Amsterdam is well-known for its vibrant nightlife – a scene that runs the gamut from the high culture of sophisticated venues for classical music, opera, theatre and dance, to the notoriously erotic and sometimes sleazy dens of the red-light district. In between are the numerous, frequently bohemian, haunts of contemporary cafe society, plus lots of cabaret venues, nightclubs and discos, featuring the latest in hiphop, techno, garage and other current sounds for youngsters.

Highlights of the regular September–May cultural season include the Holland Festival, which takes place every June. This festival is associated with events in other cities – notably The Hague, Rotterdam and Utrecht. In July and August, the somewhat avant-garde Amsterdam Arts Adventure event attracts creative types from throughout the country.

The local theatre scene is excellent, but you are unlikely to appreciate it unless you are conversant with Dutch – the language spoken in virtually all local productions. If you are a real theatre aficionado however, it is worth checking the listings and programmes during your visit, as there may well be one or two performances in English.

Amsterdam's major cinemas screen international films in their original language (with subtitles). Given the ubiquity of Hollywood productions, English-speaking cinema-goers can enjoy movies in their own language.

The nightlife venues listed in this section cover the main focal points of entertainment in Amsterdam and beyond, but there are plenty of other options on offer. For arts and entertainment listings, the VVV (local tourism association) publishes the monthly English-language magazine *What's On In Amsterdam*. There are VVV offices inside the Centraal Station building, outside the station on Stationsplein, and also at 1 Leidseplein (tel: 0900-400 4040).

You might have a look at the free, Dutch-language, monthly *Uitgaan* and several other publications published by AUB (Amsterdams Uit Buro, 21 Kleine Gartmanplantsoen, tel: 020-621 1211). Similarly worth checking out is the free *City Informatie Amsterdam*, which can be found lying around in hotel lobbies and some restaurants, and which is published twice a month.

Classical Music
Beurs van Berlage
243 Damrak
Tel: 020-627 0466
The Beurs van Berlage, the beautiful old Stock Exchange building near the Dam, dates from 1903. Transformed into a twin-hall concert venue, it is today the home of the Netherlands Philharmonic Orchestra and the Netherlands Chamber Orchestra, both of which are worth hearing.

Concertgebouw
2–6 Concertgebouwplein
Tel: 020-671 8345
The prosaically named Concertgebouw (Concert Building) is one of the world's most illustrious concert halls. The city's leading venue for classical music, it is home to the renowned Concertgebouw Orchestra.

Dr Anton Philips Concertzaal
150 Spui
Tel: 070-360 9810
Behind Den Haag Centraal Station, this is home to The Hague's Residentie Orchestra.

Churches
Among the churches featuring outstanding organs – which are often utilised for recitals and chamber-music concerts – are these:

Engelse Kerk
Begijnhof
Tel: 020-624 9665

Nieuwe Kerk
Dam
Tel: 020-626 8168

Oude Kerk
Oudekerksplein
Tel: 020-625 8284

Waalse Kerk
Walenpleintje
Tel: 020-623 2074

Opera and Dance
Muziektheater
22 Waterlooplein
Tel: 020-625 5455
An excellent setting for ballet and opera. The construction of the building was controversial but it has become a star in the cultural firmament, home of both the Netherlands Opera and the Netherlands Dance Theatre.

Stadsschouwburg
26 Leidseplein
Tel: 020-624 2311
The opera and dance productions staged here tend to be more avant-garde than the shows at the Muziektheater.

The Hague
Lucent Dans Theater
152 Spui
Tel: 070-360 4930
This is a modern venue where the esteemed Nederlands Dans Theater's three troupes perform.

Theatre
Carré
115–25 Amstel
Tel: 020-622 5225
This large theatre situated on the banks of the Amstel features well-known international music acts. The musicals may be in Dutch or in English, with many of the latter performed by touring companies from London and New York.

Nieuwe de la Mar Theater
404 Marnixstraat
Tel: 020-623 3462
Mainstream theatre, with plays usually in Dutch but occasionally in English.

Theater Bellevue
90 Leidsekade
Tel: 020-624 7248
Plays on an intimate scale. Seasonal programmes include English-language productions from time to time.

Dance Clubs
Akhnaton
25 Nieuwezijds Kolk
Tel: 020-624 3396
Offers an eclectic range of music, attracting a diverse crowd. Live jazz and salsa top the bill.

Dansen bij Jansen
11 Handboogstraat
Tel: 020-620 1779
This is a consistently popular student disco. It manages to maintain its appeal with the ever-changing, youthful in-crowd.

Above: the Muziektheater is an excellent venue for opera and dance

Melkweg
234 Lijnbaansgracht
Tel: 020-624 1777
Located in a former dairy factory, the Melkweg (Milky Way) is a long-established venue which is something of a relic from the flower-power, marijuana-fuelled days of the 1960s. Now the hippie aesthetic has given way to multimedia chic, and the Melkweg features a dance floor, a theatre, a lecture hall and a cinema.

Seymour Likely Too
161 Nieuwezijds Voorburgwal
Tel: 020-420 5663
This unusually named venue offers appropriately hip music in an avant-garde location.

Soul Kitchen
32 Amstelstraat
Tel: 020-620 2333
As its name suggests, this club serves up tasty soul sounds. Other kinds of music are also on offer, but the main emphasis is on the sounds of the 1960s and 1970s.

West Pacific
Westergasfabriek
8–10 Haarlemmerweg
Tel: 020-488 7778
Dance to funky Latin and hip-hop rhythms at this trendy spot in a sprawling, redeveloped gasworks complex situated to the west of Centraal Station.

Jazz and Blues
Alto Jazz Café
115 Korte Leidsedwarsstraat
Tel: 020-626 3249
One of the city's most popular and friendly jazz venues.

Bimhuis
73 Oudeschans
Tel: 020-623 3373
Cool and laid-back, Bimhuis features modern jazz and improvised music, with locals and aspiring talents getting their chance early in the week.

Bourbon Street
6 Leidsekruisstraat
Tel: 020-623 3440
Bourbon Street is highly recommended for those who like their jazz to be 'straight ahead' or mainstream.

Maloe Melo
163 Lijnbaansgracht
Tel: 020-420 4592
Mellow blues played nightly in a suitably smoky atmosphere.

Rock and Pop Concerts
Amsterdam ArenA
Bijlmermeer (Amsterdam Zuidoost)
Tel: 020-311 1313
Since it opened in 1996, the quite stupendous stadium of the Ajax Amsterdam football team has become a venue for big-name concerts from time to time.

Experimental Music
De IJsbreker
23 Weesperzijde
Tel: 020-668 1805
This cafe-venue beside the River Amstel is the place to go for the latest in pioneering musical sounds and forms.

Cabaret
Boom Chicago
Leidseplein Theater, 12 Leidseplein
Tel: 020-530 7300
Fast-paced, usually English-language, comedy theatre that satirises the leading international news of the day. Bring your sense of humour.

Left: Damrak, near Centraal Station

Casinos
Holland Casino Amsterdam
64 Max Euweplein
Tel: 020-521 1111
The city's only legal casino. Formal dress and passport for entry. Roulette, blackjack, punto banco (a version of baccarat) and poker. Or feed the slot machines.

Holland Casino Zandvoort
7 Badhuisplein
Tel: 023-574 0574
Like the Amsterdam branch but on the coast.

Cinemas
Bellevue
400 Marnixstraat
Tel: 020-620 8417
Two screens in a street off Leidseplein.

Calypso
402 Marnixstraat
Tel: 020-620 8417
Two-screen neighbour of the Bellevue.

City
13 Kleine Gartmanplantsoen
Tel: 020-623 4579
Seven screens not far from Leidseplein.

The Movies
161 Haarlemmerdijk
Tel: 020-638 6016
Alternatives to Hollywood blockbusters.

Tuschinski
26 Reguliersbreestraat
Tel: 020-626 2633
Six-screen cinema in a building whose fine Art Deco interior is itself worth an Oscar. Just off Rembrandtplein.

Brown Cafes
Amsterdam's brown cafés (traditional bars) are an integral part of the city's nightlife. The following are some of the best.

Café Chris
42 Bloemstraat
Tel: 020-624 5942
Located not far from Westermarkt, this cafe dates from 1624. Today's clientele, like much of the city, is fairly bohemian.

De Druif
83 Rapenburg
Tel: 020-624 4530
Situated on the waterfront in the Oosterdok area, this popular local cafe opened in 1631.

Hoppe
18–20 Spui
Tel: 020-420 4420
Friendly, popular cafe from 1670.

In de Wildeman
3 Kolksteeg
Tel: 020-638 2348
In an alley off Nieuwezijds Voorburgwal, this 1690 brown cafe, originally a liqueur distillery, has an extensive range of beers.

De Karpershoek
2 Martelaarsgracht
Tel: 020-624 7886
Traditional, former sailors' den dating to 1629, De Karpershoek has a sand-covered floor. Situated opposite Centraal Station.

't Smalle
12 Egelantiersgracht
Tel: 020-623 9617
Pavement and canal-side terraces.

Trendy Cafes
Dante
320 Spuistraat
Tel: 020-638 8839
Includes an art gallery where, every month, a new modern-art exhibition is displayed.

Schiller
36 Rembrandtplein
Tel: 020-624 9864
Friendly, trendy temple of good taste.

Left: preparing a restorative beverage

CALENDAR OF EVENTS

March
In honour of the 1345 Miracle of the Host, Catholics parade in the *Stille Omgang* (Silent Procession), beginning at the Dam on the nearest Sunday to the 15th.
For details of the **Amsterdam Blues Festival** at De Meervaart, tel: 020-610 7393.
The Keukenhof Garden at Lisse is open for the **tulip season** (Mar–May).

April
On **Good Friday**, the Concertgebouw Orchestra plays Bach's *The Passion According to Saint Matthew* in its concert hall.
National Museum Weekend (usually on a mid-month weekend) features free or reduced-rate entry to most city museums.
Koninginnedag (the Queen's official birthday) on the 30th is celebrated throughout the country. A street market and music festival bring Amsterdam to a standstill. Wear orange.

May
Bevrijdingsdag (Liberation Day) on 5 May celebrates the defeat of the Nazis. The revelries in Amsterdam are comparable to those on *Koninginnedag*.

June
The Vondelpark's open-air **theatre season** runs from June–Sept.
The **Holland Festival**, a month-long programme of music, theatre, opera, film and dance focuses on Amsterdam, The Hague, Rotterdam and Utrecht. For details, tel: 020-627 6566.
The **World Roots Festival** brings world music, dance, films, exhibitions and workshops to the Melkweg, on variable dates. For more information, tel: 020-624 1777.
Kunst RAI (Arts RAI) at the RAI Exhibition centre (variable dates) showcases the art of a different country every year. For details, contact the RAI, tel: 020-549 1212.

July
Cultural events under the umbrella of the **Arts Adventure** programme take place in July and Aug. The idea is to extend the cultural season into these hitherto dormant

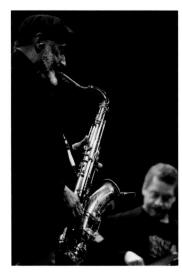

months, when the city is full of tourists. Informal music, theatre and dance events are frequently held at open-air venues. For details contact the AUB (Amsterdam Uit Buro), tel: 020-621 1211.

August
The resort of Zandvoort swings to the sound of live jazz in its **Jazz Behind the Beach** festival, usually held in the first week of August at various venues in the town.

September
The *Bloemencorso* (Flower Parade) is an extravagant procession that begins in Aalsmeer and ends in Amsterdam, usually in the first week of the month.
The **Jordaan Festival**, a loosely-structured series of musical and performance events, takes place in this Amsterdam district in the first two weeks of the month.
The **Amsterdam City Marathon** usually takes place at the end of the month.

November
On the Saturday nearest to 17 November, the **Festival of Sint Nicolaas** is marked by a procession from Prins Hendrikkade to the city centre, featuring Nicolaas's helper, Zwarte Piet (Black Peter).

December
Holiday on Ice at the RAI Exhibition Centre.

Right: the sound of jazz

Practical
Information

GETTING THERE

By Air

Amsterdam's Schiphol Airport, some 14km (9 miles) southwest of the city, is widely considered to be among the world's best. KLM Royal Dutch Airlines is the national carrier. Most major international airlines fly to Amsterdam and there are connections from (among numerous other places) London, New York, Los Angeles, Toronto, Sydney, Auckland, Johannesburg, Bombay, Singapore, Seoul and Tokyo. For flight information, tel: 0900-0141.

There is a 24-hour rail service from Schiphol to Amsterdam Centraal Station, with up to six trains an hour at peak times. Trains also leave, though less frequently, for Amsterdam RAI Station and Amsterdam Zuid/WTC (South/World Trade Centre) Station. In all three cases, the journey time is about 20 minutes.

Taxis to the city centre depart from a rank in front of Schiphol Plaza. KLM operates a hotel shuttle bus from the airport, which serves 16 city-centre hotels (all of which are close to many other hotels), every 20–30 minutes from 7am to 9.30pm.

By Rail

There are regular international services to Amsterdam Centraal Station from Paris, Brussels, Cologne, Berlin and a number of cities in eastern Europe, Switzerland and Italy. In addition, the Thalys high-speed train connects the city with Brussels and Paris (reservations are mandatory).

By Road

Four EU-designated motorways converge on the city from Belgium and Germany: the E19, E22, E35 and E231.

By Sea

DFDS Seaways operates a passenger service with vessels sailing every second day between Newcastle and IJmuiden near Amsterdam; P&O North Sea Ferries has one sailing a day between Hull and Rotterdam Europoort; and Stena Line has two sailings a day between Harwich and Hoek van Holland near Rotterdam.

TRAVEL ESSENTIALS

When to Visit

The best times for a trip to Amsterdam is in spring, summer and early autumn (Apr–Oct). The weather is at its best and the museums and other attractions have longer opening hours. Spring is the time to see the glorious tulip displays in the nearby bulb fields. Winter can also be good, particularly if the canals freeze: bring your skates and see the city of canals in a different guise.

Visas and Passports

EU citizens do not need a visa. Citizens of most other European countries, the US, Canada, Australia, New Zealand, Japan and some other places do not need a visa for stays of up to three months. Citizens of other countries must have a visa. If in doubt, check with the Dutch embassy or consulate in your home country, or country of departure, or with your travel agent or airline.

Customs

There are no currency restrictions. EU citizens can import for personal use up to 800 cigarettes, 400 cigars, or 400g tobacco; 90 litres of wine; 10 litres of spirits.

Left: canal boats give a fine perspective
Right: a much faster mode of transport

Non-EU citizens can import duty-free a maximum of: 200 cigarettes, 50 cigars, or 50g of tobacco; 2 litres of wine, or 1 litre of spirits. If purchasing flower bulbs you should be aware that the majority of countries forbid the import of flower bulbs without an official phytosanitary certificate – many vendors sell bulbs with a certificate on the label.

Weather

The climate is generally temperate. July and August can be hot, but even in summer, Amsterdam, benefiting from its proximity to the North Sea, often enjoys a cooling breeze, and occasionally some rain.

Winters are frequently cold enough for the canals to freeze over to the extent that ice-skaters can glide across them. The average summer temperature is 16°C (60°F), although it can soar to 30°C (86°F). In winter the average temperature is 3°C (37°F), but it can fall to -20°C (-4°F).

Clothing

Even in summer it's a good idea to bring a sweater or cardigan because the evenings can be cool. Moreover, due to Amsterdam's proximity to the sea, the weather can change quickly. An umbrella is a vital accessory at almost any time.

Warm clothes are essential in winter. In most situations, even if dining at a high-class restaurant or attending the opera, casual outfits are acceptable. Businesspeople often dress informally; Dutch business people tend to adopt a more stylish appearance than many of their foreign counterparts.

Electricity

The unit of electricity in the Netherlands is 220 volts AC. Hotels may have a 110-volt or 120-volt outlet for shavers.

Time

The country operates on Central European Standard Time, with Daylight Saving Time coming into play from late March to late October. (Daylight Saving Time is GMT plus one hour in winter, plus two hours in summer.) For most of the year, the Netherlands is one hour ahead of the UK, and six hours ahead of the US's Eastern Standard Time.

GETTING ACQUAINTED

Geography

Amsterdam, like most of the Netherlands, is uniformly flat and lies below sea level – dykes protect the land from the ravages of the North Sea. The Dam district constitutes the heart of the city. North of the Dam is Centraal Station, which is also the main tram, bus and metro terminus. A horseshoe of concentric canals – Singel, Herengracht, Keizersgracht and Prinsengracht – forms a semi-circle around the Dam, culminating at the River Amstel in the east.

Government and Economy

The city council is headed by a mayor whose power invariably entitles him to set his stamp on the city's social and economic affairs. Don't get carried away by Amsterdam's reputation for free living. Nowadays, that anything-goes lifestyle is more a product of the residents' wealth and liberalism than of hippie values and soft drugs.

As a result of assiduous promotion and heavy investment, the Amsterdam-Schiphol Airport district has become a booming enterprise zone, as can be seen from the extensive suburban business developments. Any number of multinational corporations have located their European headquarters and distribution operations here.

Religion

The Netherlands is predominantly Calvinist, with the Dutch Reformed Church being the most popular denomination. There is a substantial Roman Catholic minority (or majority in the south). But if you visit any

Right: a city of fine architectural detail

church in Amsterdam during a Sunday service you will find that religion is honoured more often in the breach than the observance.

How Not to Offend

It is hard to offend Amsterdammers, whose approach to life is that whatever works for you is okay by them. But even this live-and-let-live attitude has its limits. The locals don't like boorish, loud and aggressive behaviour, nor do they take kindly to being treated like servants. Like the majority of Dutch people they are proud of their nation – if not in a shallow, flag-waving sense – and don't like too much criticism of its ways.

Avoiding Trouble

You certainly should not trust the junkie in the red-light district who wants to take a photo of you with your own camera, nor should you give credence to most of the hard-luck stories you may hear at Centraal Station from people whose money has mysteriously vanished and who need someone to pay for their ticket home. Watch out for pickpockets in all busy places, especially at Centraal Station and on crowded buses and trams.

Population

The population of Amsterdam stands at about 750,000, one-third of whom are either foreigners or from ethnic minorities. The old Dutch colonies of Indonesia and Surinam used to be the main sources of immigration. Nowadays, Amsterdam is a real melting pot, with immigrants from many countries.

MONEY MATTERS

Currency

In January 2002, like most EU nations, Holland adopted the euro currency, thereby consigning the Dutch guilder to history. There are 100 cents in a euro. Notes come in denominations of €5, €10, €20, €50, €100, €200 and €500. There are also 1-cent, 2-cent, 5-cent, 10-cent, 20-cent, €1 and €2 coins.

Credit Cards and Cheques

The major international credit and charge cards are accepted by a wide range of businesses. Traveller's cheques should be

exchanged for euros at banks, foreign exchange offices, or hotels.

Cash Machines

There are automatic cash-dispensers (ATMs) dotted all over the city. Many can be accessed by foreign bank cards and credit cards, some also by the major charge cards.

Tipping

Taxis, most restaurants, hairdressers, etc include a tip in the bill as a service charge. Staff still appreciate a tip of 5–10 percent for good service, although you won't be publicly humiliated for not leaving one. At many public toilets you have to deposit 25 or 50 cents in the attendant's saucer.

Taxes

Non-EU residents are entitled to a refund on the value-added tax (BTW) paid on purchases of around €150 or more in one shop on one day. The goods must be exported from the EU within three months. Ask for a tax-free shopping receipt when you pay, and a leaflet that explains the scheme.

Money Changers

The 'commission' charged by some money-changing establishments may leave you with the feeling that you have been mugged. The GWK (Grenswisselkantoor) exchanges at airports, main railway stations, and some border motorway services offer the best deals. Banks are also reliable. In other locations, including hotels, ask about the rates and commission in advance.

Above: a welcoming taxi driver

practical information

GETTING AROUND

Walking
As demonstrated by our suggested itineraries, the best way to get around in Amsterdam is by foot, with public transport – especially trams – and bicycles providing ancillary back-up. The city centre is small enough to make walking the most practical option, and there are plenty of relatively quiet streets and canal sides for getting away from the crowds and traffic.

Taxis
Officially, you are not allowed to wave down taxis in the street, but nowadays they usually stop if you do. Your best bet is either to wait at one of the taxi ranks scattered around the city, for example at Centraal Station, the Dam, Leidseplein and Rembrandtplein, or telephone Taxi Centrale, tel: 020-677 7777.

Public Transport
The efficient public transport network of trams, buses and metro trains operated by GVB Amsterdam provides a bewildering array of fare options, the simplest of which is the *dagkaart* (day ticket), which gives unlimited use on the day – and night – of purchase. You can also buy a *strippenkaart* (strip ticket) with 8, 15 or 45 strips (the more strips, the less each one costs) which must be punched on the vehicle, by machine, driver or conductor.

The city is divided into public-transport zones. Punch one strip more than the number of zones in which you will be travelling – two strips for one zone; three strips for two zones, etc. The ticket is valid for unlimited transfers for one hour after the time stamped on it. Although you can buy tickets on trams and buses, they are cheaper at rail and metro ticket counters, newsagents and VVV (local tourism offices).

Tram/Bus
There are 16 tram routes, 10 of which begin and end at Centraal Station. The routes are complemented by extensive urban and regional bus services. The lives of locals and visitors alike are made easier by maps of the city's public transport network that are posted at most tram and bus stops.

Metro/Train
There is a limited but fast and modern metro service to outlying housing schemes and the southern suburbs. This is not of much use for getting around within the city centre. The train service is good for a few destinations beyond the city, but less so in the city itself.

Driving
Amsterdam has taken preventive measures to stem the flow of traffic into the old city centre. Parking is expensive, and illegally parked cars are clamped or towed away by the hyperefficient parking authority. In short, it is not a good idea to bring your car.

Neither is hiring a car a good way to see the city's attractions. But if you do choose this option, try either of the following:
• Hertz: Schiphol Airport and 333 Overtoom, tel: 020-612 2441
• Avis: Schiphol Airport and 7 Hogehilweg, tel: 020-430 9611.

Cycling
Given the popularity of cycling in the Netherlands, it's not surprising that cyclists in Amsterdam are regarded as privileged road users, as you will if you are driving a car in the city. You can hire bikes from some hotels and train stations, or try:
• MacBike, 2 Mr Visserplein, tel: 020-620 0985 and also 220 Marnixstraat, tel: 020-626 6964;
• Damstraat Rent-a-Bike, 22–24 Damstraat, tel: 020-625 5029.

Cycle carefully – the streets are full of foreign visitors who, having no experience of dealing with bikes en masse, are liable to step out in front of you without looking.

Right: informal marketing for bike-hire

On the Water

In addition to taking tours by canal boat and water-bike, you can take advantage of the canals *qua* thoroughfares. To get around the city by canal boat, try one of the following:
• Canal Bus, tel: 020-623 9886, operates two city-centre routes.
• Museumboot, tel: 020-622 2181, connects some of the major museums by boat.
• Watertaxi, tel: 020-530 1090.

HOURS AND HOLIDAYS

Business Hours

Banks are open Mon–Fri 9am–4 or 5pm. Shops are usually open Mon–Sat 8.30 or 9am–6pm, with late-night shopping Thur until 9pm. Numerous shops are also open on Sun, while some stay closed on Mon mornings. There are plenty of *avondwinkels* (local late-night shops) and 'corner stores' that stay open until 10pm or later.

Public Holidays

New Year	1 January
Good Friday	variable
Easter Monday	variable
Koninginnedag (Queen's Birthday)	
	30 April
Bevrijdingsdag (Liberation Day)	
	5 May
Ascension Day	6th Thursday after Easter
Whit Monday	7th Monday after Easter
Christmas Day	25 December
Boxing Day	26 December

Market Days

Albert Cuyp Market (general): Albert Cuyp-straat, Mon–Sat.
Art Market: Thorbeckeplein, Mar–Dec: Sun.
Bio Market (organic fruit and vegetables): Noordermarkt, Sat morning.
Bloemenmarkt (flowers): Singel, Mon–Sat.
Garden Market: Amstelveld, Sun.
Textiles and Garment Market: Noorder-markt, Mon morning.
Flea Market (antiques and second-hand books): Waterlooplein, daily (summer: Sun only).
Stamps and Coins Market: Nieuwezijds Voorburgwal (behind the Royal Palace), Wed and Sat, 9am–1pm.

ACCOMMODATION

Hotels

Amsterdam is well served by accommodation options in all price categories. In recent years the emphasis has been on the top end of the market – a trend the municipality is trying to reverse. At peak times in summer, and during the spring tulip season, it can be difficult to find rooms in low- and moderately-priced hotels, so book your accommodation in advance if possible. Should you arrive at such times without a room, your best bet is to go to the VVV (local tourism office) at Centraal Station: there are two offices here – one inside, the other outside the station – and the staff at both should be able to find a room and make reservations for you.

The price categories listed below are for a double room at roughly the following rates:
$ = €30–75
$$ = €75–150
$$$ = €150–220
$$$$ = over €220.

American Hotel
97 Leidsekade
Tel: 020-556 3000
Fax: 020-556 3001
www.intercontinenti.com
A monument protected by the city on account of its Art Nouveau architecture, this hotel is also a testament to style. The staff's laid-back approach makes it popular with a wide range of people. A visit to its Café Américain is recommended. $$$$

Right: Café Américain at the American Hotel

Amstel Inter-Continental Amsterdam
1 Prof. Tulpplein
Tel: 020-622 6060
Fax: 020-622 5808
www.intercontinenti.com
Built in 1867, the Amstel overlooks the River Amstel. Replete with marble, chandeliers and oceans of genuine Delft blue porcelain, it constitutes the ultimate in luxury. Its French La Rive restaurant has earned two prestigious Michelin stars. $$$$

Golden Tulip Barbizon Palace
59–72 Prins Hendrikkade
Tel: 020-327 1177
Fax: 020-624 3353
www.goldentulip.com
A superbly equipped hotel built alongside old canal houses opposite Centraal Station. The ideal option if you are looking for more than just a touch of modern luxury. $$$$.

Grand Hotel Krasnapolsky
9 Dam Square
Tel: 020-554 9111
Fax: 020-554 7010
www.krasnapolsky.com
Founded in 1866 but now modernised, the Kras is a local institution. Its Winter Garden restaurant is the epitome of Victorian-era elegance. Fine location at the Dam. $$$$

Hôtel de l'Europe
2–8 Nieuwe Doelenstraat
Tel: 020-531 1777
Fax: 020-531 1778
www.leurope.nl
An elegant river-side hotel dating from 1896 with a distinctive red-and-white facade and a grand sense of style. The plush guest rooms have modern furnishings and amenities. The Excelsior restaurant is one of the most highly regarded in town. $$$$

Estheréa
303–309 Singel
Tel: 020-624 5146
Fax: 020-623 9001
www.estherea.nl
With its beautiful canal side location, the Estheréa combines old Amsterdam charm and 21st-century facilities. One of the best value-for-money options in the city. $$$

Pulitzer Sheraton
315–331 Prinsengracht
Tel: 020-523 5235
Fax: 020-627 6753
www.sheraton.com
A terrace of 17th- and 18th-century canal houses converted into a hotel of charm and character. The furnishings are beautiful, the bedrooms – overlooking canals or gardens – sophisticated. The French De Goudsbloem restaurant is appropriately classy. $$$

Radisson SAS
17 Rusland
Tel: 020-623 1231
Fax: 020-520 8200
www.radisson.com
Set deep in the heart of Old Amsterdam, this stylish Scandinavian hotel offers an eclectic range of designs in its guest rooms. $$$

Schiller
26–36 Rembrandtplein
Tel: 020-554 0700
Fax: 020-624 0098
www.goldentuliphotels.nl/gtschiller
As much an art gallery as a hotel, the Schiller was built in the *fin de siècle* period by an artist who filled it with his own creations and those by artists he particularly liked. The wood-panelled Café Schiller has long been one of the city's trendy hangouts. $$$

Victoria
1–5 Damrak
Tel: 020-627 1166
Fax: 020-627 4259
www.parkplazaamsterdam.com
Well-located opposite Centraal Station and impervious to the street noise. A plush, option, full of character. $$$

Ambassade
335–53 Herengracht
Tel: 020-555 0222
Fax: 020-555 0277
www.ambassade-hotel.nl
An hospitable, exclusive hotel created from a series of 17th- and 18th-century canal side houses, the Ambassade features plenty of antiques and paintings, and steep – in some cases spiral – staircases. Especially popular with visiting writers. $$

Amsterdam

93–94 Damrak
Tel: 020-555 0666
Fax: 020-620 4716
www.hotelamsterdam.nl

This fine, medium-sized hotel, conveniently situated near Centraal Station, opened in 1911 but has been thoroughly modernised. The hotel's De Roode Leeuw is one of the city's best Dutch restaurants. $$

Amsterdam Wiechmann

328 Prinsengracht
Tel: 020-626 3321
Fax: 020-626 8962
www.hotelwiechmann.nl

A laid-back American owner and his Dutch wife have turned this rambling old canal-house hotel into one of the city's most welcoming addresses. You can't beat the location, and the rates are reasonable. $$

Best Western Eden

144 Amstel
Tel: 020-530 7888
Fax: 020-623 3267
www.edenhotelgroup.com

This moderately-priced river-side hotel has 410 rooms, so it might be a good bet when other hotels are fully booked. And it retains much of the character of the 17th-century merchants' homes from which it was created. Guest rooms are furnished in modern style and the Garden of Eden brasserie serves good Dutch food. $$

Bridge

107–11 Amstel
Tel: 020-623 7068
Fax: 020-624 1565
www.thebridgehotel.demon.nl

Overlooking the River Amstel, the Bridge offers space, style and a relaxed atmosphere in its 27 rooms. $$

Dikker & Thijs Fenice

444 Prinsengracht
Tel: 020-626 1212
Fax: 020-625 8986
www.dtfh.nl

Small, quiet, tasteful and full of character, this gem of a hotel is located adjacent to the busy Leidsestraat shopping street. $$

De Filosoof

6 Anna van den Vondelstraat
Tel: 020-683 3013
Fax: 020-685 3750
www.xs4all.nl/~filosoof

One of De Filosoof's greatest assets is its location – on a quiet street beside Vondelpark and within walking distance of Leidseplein and the major museums. But its main claim to singularity is its philosophical theme. The individually furnished rooms are inspired by the great thinkers, as is the owner, who is herself a philospher. A haven of comfort and good taste. $$

Jan Luyken

54–58 Jan Luykenstraat
Tel: 020-573 0730
Fax: 020-676 3841
www.janluyken.nl

A fine blend of comfort and local character, the Jan Luyken is set in a graceful residential area near the Van Gogh Museum. $$

Die Port Van Cleve

50 Nieuwezijds Voorburgwal
Tel: 020-624 4860
Fax: 020-622 0240
www.dieportvancleve.com

A recently modernised, century-old hotel to the rear of the Royal Palace. Its turreted facade remains intact. $$

Rembrandt Residence Hotel

225 Herengracht
Tel: 020-622 1727
Fax: 020-625 0630
www.bookings.nl/hotels/rembrandt

A rambling hotel that incorporates a number of old buildings, many of whose original fittings remain. Big on atmosphere, less so on most modern facilities. $$

Right: Die Port Van Cleve, now modernised

Seven Bridges
1 Reguliersgracht
Tel: 020-623 1329
A small, centrally located canal-side hotel with 10 rooms plus self-catering apartments in neighbouring houses. The atmosphere is enhanced by well-chosen furnishings and fittings, and there are good views of seven canal bridges. Beautiful gardens. $$

Vondel
8 Vondelstraat
Tel: 020-612 0120
Fax: 020-685 4321
www.srs/worldhotels.com
vondel@bhs.nl
Comfortable, well-equipped rooms and excellent value for money. Despite its off-centre location, the Vondel is convenient for the Vondelpark and the Leidseplein. $$

Acacia
251 Lindengracht
Tel: 020-622 1460
Fax: 020-638 0748
www.hotelacacia.nl
This fine small hotel in the Jordaan district has plain but comfortable guest rooms and, unusually, a pair of houseboats moored on the adjacent canal. $

De Admiraal
563 Herengracht
Tel: 020-626 2150
Fax: 020-623 4625
A friendly, homely hotel, adjacent to the pretty, tree-shaded Thorbeckeplein square, De Admiraal featured in the 1970 Alistair MacLean movie *Puppet on a Chain*. $

Amstel Botel
4 Oosterdokskade
Tel: 020-626 4247
Fax: 020-639 1952
If you're looking for an offbeat lodging option, try this floating hotel, situated between Centraal Station and the Maritime Museum. The rooms – or cabins – are clean and simple but comfortably furnished with views over the water. Late at night this location does become somewhat dubious so the Amstel Botel is not an ideal choice for single women. $

Hoksbergen
301 Singel
Tel: 020-626 6043
Fax: 020-638 3479
www.hotelhoksbergen.com
The Hoksbergen represents an uncommon combination of qualities: high-standard accommodation in a desirable, canal-side location that is good value for money. A characterful, comfortable option. $

Keizershof
618 Keizersgracht
Tel: 020-622 2855
Fax: 020-624 8412
www.vdwp.nl/keizershof
Unfortunately this wonderful little canal-side hotel has only six guest rooms, so try to book your accommodation here as far in advance as possible. The owners, the De Vries family, are most hospitable, and they take pride in providing something akin to being a home from home. $

Orfeo
14 Leidsekruisstraat
Tel: 020-623 1347
Fax: 020-620 2348
Popular with the city's many gay visitors, this hotel just off Leidseplein has simple but clean rooms and a friendly character. The breakfast dining room is a bit bland but Orfeo nevertheless represents good value. $

P. C. Hooft
63 P.C. Hooftstraat
Tel: 020-662 7107
Fax: 020-675 8961
A budget lodging on Amsterdam's most prestigious shopping street. The PC Hooft's owners rely on the simple virtues to keep their clientele satisfied. $

Parkzicht
33 Roemer Visscherstraat
Tel: 020-618 1954
Fax: 020-618 0897
Reasonable rates and a fine location overlooking the Vondelpark are Parkzicht's most pertinent assets, and it is particularly successful in attracting a young clientele. The decor is Old Dutch, the welcome friendly. $

Piet Hein

52 Vossiusstraat
Tel: 020-662 7205
Fax: 020-662 1526
www.hotelpiethein.com
Located in a converted mansion in a quiet neighbourhood beside the Vondelpar, the Piet Hein is a popular option offering comfortable accommodation. It has an adjacent annexe $

Prinsenhof

810 Prinsengracht
Tel: 020-623 1772
Fax: 020-638 3368
www.hotelprinsenhof.com
Although somewhat rough and ready in places, the Prinsenhof is constantly being improved by its enthusiastic owners. The 'casual Amsterdam' atmosphere is exactly what many travellers particularly like about the place. $

Sint Nicolaas

1a Spuistraat
Tel: 020-626 1384
Fax: 020-623 0979
www.hotelnicolaas.nl
This is a friendly and comfortable establishment conveniently situated near Centraal Station. $

Toren

164 Keizersgracht
Tel: 020-622 6352
Fax: 020-626 9705
www.toren.nl
Situated close to Westermarkt, the Toren is a canal-house hotel that occupies two neighbouring buildings. The guest rooms are clean and attractive, and most have a private bathroom. $

Van de Kasteelen

34 Frans van Mierisstraat
Tel: 020-670 6604
The Indonesian couple who own and run this hotel, not far from the Concertgebouw, have transformed it into one of the city's simple jewels. There might not be much in the way of luxurious facilities, but all the rooms are clean and offer an adequate level of comfort. $

Van Ostade Bicycle Hotel

123 Van Ostadestraat
Tel: 020-679 3452
Fax: 020-671 5213
www.etrade.nl/bicyclehotel
The young proprietors have turned commitment to environmentally-friendly transport – you can rent bikes cheaply here – into a comfortable hotel for cyclists. $

Waterfront

458 Singel
Tel: 020-421 6621
Typical of the many moderately-priced canal-side hotels, the Waterfront offers atmosphere, comfort and a reasonable level of service. $

Wynnobel

9 Vossiusstraat
Tel: 020-662 2298
Small, cheap and cheerful, family-owned hotel with views of the Vondelpark. There are no private bathrooms but the Wynnobel is conveniently situated, not far from public transport stops, shopping centres and the major museums. $

Budget Hotels & Youth Hostels

Amsterdam has a good array of hostels that are open to guests of all ages. Most offer dormitory accommodation, some provide private rooms, a few have family facilities. Those that require membership can issue you with a card on the spot.

Bob's Youth Hostel

92 Nieuwezijds Voorburgwal
Tel: 020-623 0063

Euphemia

1–9 Fokke Simonszstraat
Tel: 020-622 9045
www.euphemiahotel.com

Hans Brinker

136 Kerkstraat
Tel: 020-622 0687
www.hans-brinker.com

International Student Centre

15 Keizersgracht
Tel: 020-625 1364

NJHC City Hostel Stadsdoelen
97 Kloveniersburgwal
Tel: 020-624 6832
Fax: 020-639 1035
www.njhc.org
Situated on a canal close to the red-light district, a 10-minute walk from Dam Square.

NJHC City Hostel Vondelpark
5 Zandpad
Tel: 020-589 8996
Fax: 020-589 8955
www.njhc.org
A quiet, well-equipped hostel located in the Vondelpark, complete with recreation rooms, and a shower and toilet in every room.

Camping
Camping is permitted only on official camp sites. You can get a list of sites – most of which are easily reached by bus from Centraal Station – from VVV offices.

Vliegenbos
138 Meeuwenlaan
Tel: 020-636 8855
Fax: 020-632 2723
Well-situated in 25 ha (60 acres) of woods, just a short ride from the centre. Offers cabin and tent accommodation.

The following three camp sites are rather inaccessible but the sites' managers will fax directions on request.

De Badhoeve
10 Uitdammerdijk
Tel/fax: 020-490 4294

Gaaspercamping
7 Loosdrechtdreef
Tel: 020-696 7326
Fax: 020-696 9369

Zeeburg
20 Zuiderdijk
Tel: 020-694 4430
Fax: 020-694 6238

HEALTH AND EMERGENCIES

Pharmacies
A list of out-of-hours pharmacies is posted on the front of every *apotheek* (pharmacy).

Right: toddlers of the city unite

Medical/Dental Services
In the case of severe accidents, tel: 112. For less urgent cases, standby doctors and dentists can be reached 24 hours a day at the Centraal Medische Dienst (Central Medical Service), tel: 020-592 3434.

Crime/Trouble
Amsterdam is not particularly violent but, as is the case in most major Western cities, crime is a problem. Exercise caution in the red-light district and beware of thieves and pickpockets in crowded areas especially.

Lost Property
In the case of possessions lost on any city transport, contact the Lost Property Office at 11 Waterlooplein, tel: 020-559 8005. For items lost on trains or at railway stations, tel:020-557 8544.

Police
In emergencies, tel: 112.

Toilets
Public toilets are rare. Many restaurant and bar toilets charge a small fee.

COMMUNICATIONS AND NEWS

Post
PTT (post office) opening hours are Mon–Fri 9am–6pm. The post office at 250 Singel is also open Sat 9am–3pm.

Telephone
The country code for The Netherlands is 31. The area code for Amsterdam is 020 from

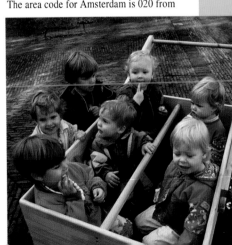

elsewhere in the country, 20 from abroad. Card-phones have replaced the majority of coin-operated phones. *Telekaarten* (phone cards) cost €5, €10 and €20 from post offices, railway stations and newspaper vendors. To call abroad, dial 00 + country code + area code + subscriber number.

Media

The *International Herald Tribune* and some British broadsheet newspapers are widely available. Cable television offers British and American networks, including the BBC and CNN. BBC Radio 4 can be picked up with good reception on long wave, and the BBC World Service and the Voice of America are both available.

USEFUL INFORMATION

Disabled

Services for disabled people are better than in most European countries. Museums and other public buildings usually have access for wheelchairs. Some trams and the metro network also provide this service.

Children

Amsterdam offers lots of attractions and facilities for children. The following attractions are all relatively child-friendly, depending on the age (and temperament) of the children concerned.

Holland Experience, Joodenbreestraat/ Waterlooplein, tel: 020-422 2233. A multimedia introduction to Holland.

NEMO (NewMetropolis Science and Technology Centre), 2 Oosterdok, tel: 0900-919 1100. Interactive science museum.

Intersphere Laser Games, 194 Prins Hendrikkade, tel: 020-622 4809. Futuristic combat for the older, more macho, child.

Kindermuseum, 2 Linnaeusstraat, tel: 020-568 8300. Part of the Tropenmuseum that is dedicated to children.

Madame Tussaud, 20 Dam, tel: 020-622 9949. Amsterdam branch of the international institution, featuring waxwork models of famous personalities.

Tram-museum Amsterdam, Haarlemmermeer Station, 264 Amstelveenseweg, tel: 020-673 7538. For the young tram-spotter.

Maps

The map accompanying this book highlights the attractions featured in the itineraries. See the laminated *Insight Fleximap: Amsterdam* or, for several maps of the city in one, *Insight Travel Map: Amsterdam*.

The VVV tourist office produces a small map and some hotels provide free maps. You can buy maps at newsagents, book stores and souvenir shops.

Museums

In addition to the museums described in the itineraries, the following might be of interest:

Allard-Pierson Museum (Archaeology), 127 Oude Turfmarkt, tel: 020-525 2556.

Amstelkring (Catholic), 40 Oudezijds Voorburgwal, tel: 020-624 6604.

Aviodome (Aviation), 201 Westelijke Randweg, Schiphol Airport, tel: 020-604 1521.

Bijbels Museum (The Bible), 366 Herengracht, tel: 020-624 7949.

Filmmuseum (Cinema), 3 Vondelpark, tel: 020-589 1400.

Heineken Reception Centre (Brewery), 78 Stadhouderskade, tel: 020-523 9666.

Koffie- en Thee Museum (Coffee and Tea), 67 Warmoesstraat, tel: 020-624 0683.

Sexmuseum Amsterdam Venustempel (Erotica), 18 Damrak, tel: 020-622 8376.

Verzetsmuseum (Resistance Movement), 63 Lekstraat, tel: 020-644 9797.

Werf 't Kromhout (Shipyard), 147 Hoogte Kadijk, tel: 020-627 6777.

Language

Dutch is spoken everywhere, although there are lots of local dialects, especially in rural areas. The majority of Dutch people speak at least some English, many speak it well, and an impressive number are fluent.

SPORT

Bowling

Knijn Bowling, 3 Scheldeplein, tel: 020-664 2211.

Fitness Centres

Centre Jansen, 109–11 Rokin, tel: 020-626 9366.

Sporting Club Leidseplein, 18 Korte Leidsedwarsstraat, tel: 020-620 6631.

Golf
Sloten Golf Course, 1045 Sloterweg, tel: 020-614 2402.
Waterland Golf Course, 141 Buiksloter-meerdijk, tel: 020-636 1010.

Ice Skating
Jaap Edenbaan, 64 Radioweg, tel: 020-694 9894.
In winter it is often possible to skate on frozen canals.

Riding
Amsterdamse Manege, 25 Nieuwe Kalfjes-laan, tel: 020-643 1342.

Swimming
Marnixbad, 5 Marnixplein, tel: 020-625 4843.
De Mirandabad, 9 De Mirandalaan, tel: 020-642 8080.

Tennis
Amstelpark Tenniscentre, 8 Koenenkade, Amsterdamse Bos, tel: 020-644 5436.

Squash
Squash City, Ketelmarkerstraat, tel: 020-626 7883.

USEFUL ADDRESSES

Tourist Offices
The VVV (Vereniging voor Vremdelingen Verkeer) local tourism offices are friendly, helpful and efficient. VVV Amsterdam has offices at Centraal Station (one inside, beside the reservations hall, the other outside on Stationsplein); 1 Leidseplein; and at the corner of Stadionplein. For information from VVV Amsterdam, tel: 0900-400 4040.

Netherlands Tourist Information has an office in the arrivals hall of Schiphol Plaza at Schiphol Airport. Other tourist offices are:

Haarlem
VVV Zuid-Kennemerland, 1 Stationsplein, tel: 0900-616 1600, fax 023-534 0537.

Zandvoort
VVV Zandvoort, 1 Schoolplein, tel: 023-571 7947, fax 023-571 7003, www.vvvzk.nl.

The Hague
VVV Den Haag, Koningin Julianaplein, tel: 0900-340 3505, fax: 070-347 2102, www.denhaag.nl.

Scheveningen
VVV Scheveningen, 1134 Gevers Deynootweg, tel: 0900-340 3505, fax: 070-361 5494, www.denhaag.nl.

To make hotel reservations in advance, contact the Netherlands Reservations Centre, PO Box 404, 2260 AK Leidschendam, tel: 070-320 2500; fax: 070-320 2611.

City Tours
Artifex (with guides): 342 Herengracht, tel: 020-620 8112.
Yellow Bike (bicycle tours): 9 Nieuwezijds Kolk, tel: 020-620 6940.
Holland International Excursions (through-out Holland): 6 Dam, tel: 020-551 2800.

INSIGHT GUIDES

Insight Guide: Amsterdam. Indispensible guide to the city with fascinating features, stunning photos and updated travel tips.
Compact Guide:Amsterdam and *Compact Guide: Holland.* Concise, convenient pocket books; troves of vital information.
Insight Guide:Holland. All facets of the nation comprehensively, vividly described and illustrated in user-friendly terms.

Above: friendly advice from a VVV office

INSIGHT
Pocket Guides

Insight Pocket Guides pioneered a new approach to guidebooks, introducing the concept of the authors as "local hosts" who would provide readers with personal recommendations, just as they would give honest advice to a friend who came to stay. They also included a full-size pull-out map. Now, to cope with the needs of the 21st century, new editions in this growing series are being given a new look to make them more practical to use, and restaurant and hotel listings have been greatly expanded.

☆ INSIGHT GUIDES

The world's largest collection of visual travel guides

Now in association with

ACKNOWLEDGEMENTS

Photography

David Beatty/Apa	77
Anne Frank Museum	24B
Guglielmo Galvin/Apa	1, 2/3, 6T, 7T/B, 21, 23, 26T, 28T/B, 29, 30T/B, 31, 34T/B, 36, 39B, 41T/B, 45, 46, 47, 48, 52, 53, 54, 57, 58, 59, 61, 62, 63, 67, 68, 69, 70, 71, 72, 74, 75, 76, 79, 81, 83,84, 86, 89, 91
Rijkmuseum	5, 32
Bill Wassman	6B, 25, 26B, 27, 39T, 42, 43, 44, 51, 60, 64T/B, 65, 73, 80,
Guglielmo Galvin/Apa	Cover
The Netherlands Board of Tourism	Back cover
Maria Donnelly	Cartography
Tanvir Virdee	Cover Design

INDEX